Gender and the Interpretation of
Classical Myth

CLASSICAL INTER/FACES

Also available

Lucretius and the Modern World
W.R. Johnson

Pity Transformed
David Konstan

Plato's Progeny
Melissa Lane

Translating Words, Translating Cultures
Lorna Hardwick

GENDER AND THE INTERPRETATION OF CLASSICAL MYTH

Lillian E. Doherty

Duckworth

This impression 2003
First published in 2001 by
Gerald Duckworth & Co. Ltd.
61 Frith Street, London W1D 3JL
Tel: 020 7434 4242
Fax: 020 7434 4420
inquiries@duckworth-publishers.co.uk
www.ducknet.co.uk

A catalogue record for this book is available
from the British Library

ISBN 0 7156 3042 3

Printed and bound in Great Britain by
Antony Rowe Ltd, Eastbourne

Contents

Acknowledgments

My deep thanks to my Chair, Judith P. Hallett, and to the other members of the Classics Department at the University of Maryland, for their moral support and willingness to let me take a semester's leave during the writing of this book. For specific suggestions and brainstorming, thanks to Judith Hallett, Gregory Staley, and Eva Stehle. Thanks to Hugh Lee for administering a myth questionnaire to his class. To Maryland colleagues outside my department – Pamela Alexander of Psychology, Katie King of Women's Studies, Bill Stuart of Anthropology – thanks for help with bibliography and specific questions.

For generous responses to miscellaneous inquiries, thanks to John Miles Foley, Wendy Doniger, Richard Martin, Barbara McManus, Gregory Nagy, Annabel Robinson, Seth Schein, Alan Shapiro, Aaron Tate, and Adrienne Zihlman.

For permission to quote from an unpublished abstract, thanks to Ann Suter.

For an invitation to lecture on the topic of Chapter 3, and for helpful feedback after my talk, thanks to Nancy Felson and the Classics faculty at the University of Georgia.

For help in my investigations of children's literature, thanks to Margaret Coughlan of the Library of Congress; to Maria Salvador of the District of Columbia Public Library; to Dr Bruce Ronda of Colorado State University; and above all to Sue Jagger and Victoria Velsey of Georgetown Day School.

For permitting me to pose an extra question on the 2001 version of the Medusa Myth Exam, thanks to the members of the Exam Committee, especially Matt Webb.

For valuable feedback on early drafts of the manuscript, thanks to Elise Brand, Denise McCoskey, and my mother, Rosemary Jantzen Doherty.

For their faith that I was the person to write this book, and for their help along the way, thanks to Susanna Braund, Paul Cartledge, and Deborah Blake.

And thanks to Harvey, for being there.

August 2001   Lillian E. Doherty

Preface

Classical Myths in Contemporary Culture

Is classical Greek and Roman mythology still a part of the common culture of Europe and the Americas at the turn of the twenty-first century? If so, what functions does it serve? In particular, how is it related to our gender system – the nexus of symbols, norms and roles that structure our gender relationships? Finally, how do its functions in our world compare with those it filled for the ancient cultures that first produced it? This book is one 'classicist's' answer – or set of answers – to these questions.

It can be argued that the notion of a 'common culture' is itself obsolete. Europe and its former colonies no longer share a widely-known body of traditional stories. The Bible and some classical authors (notably Vergil and Ovid) provided such a 'canon' for many centuries, at least to the educated classes, but even the Bible is no longer widely read. Most people now have access to electronic media and share knowledge of certain television programmes, music videos, and films, but these are not traditional and have little chance of becoming so.

Yet the mythologies of the past have never been more popular – or, arguably, more widely known – than they are today. Greek and Roman myths are among the most prominent, thanks to several television series and to Disney films based on Hercules and Atlantis. Great numbers of children's books and comic books on mythic themes are in circulation. Enrolment in mythology courses is soaring.

How are we to reconcile these two apparently conflicting trends? My answer is that, in the phrase of Marcel Detienne, myths are 'good to think with'.[1] They differ from newly created fictions in having the weight of tradition behind them. Yet they are highly flexible: when closely examined, the versions in circulation today often vary widely, not only from ancient versions but from one another. They have the virtue of combining strangeness with familiarity. They draw us in with the lure of the exotic, yet do not pose overt threats to our assumptions about the structure of the family or of society. Thus they offer a safe space in which to ponder these assumptions and experiment with variations of them.

Myths have the glamour of strangeness, based on the remoteness of their settings in time and space and on the improbability – hence the drama – of their events. Monsters and magic, gods and goddesses, larger-than-life human figures, and reversals of expectations in the stories give scope to the imagination. As in folk and fairy tales, realism is often suspended in favour of wish-fulfilment: Perseus kills the dragon and marries Andromeda; Penelope holds out against more than a hundred suitors until Odysseus returns. When the stories end tragically, the presence of exotic details may blunt the pain or keep it at a safe distance from the audience. Yet the story patterns are based on conflicts that arise within the familiar frameworks of the patriarchal family and of a wider society in which authority and property are still distributed on patriarchal lines.

In these respects, the relationship between myth and society has not changed since ancient times. Even for the audiences of Greece and Rome, the myths were set in the remote past of the Bronze Age, a period the classical Greeks rather accurately estimated to have ended 800 years before their own time. (For the Romans of the early imperial age – Ovid's day – the gap was 1,200 years.) Moreover, ancient and 'traditional' though they were, the myths never existed in single authoritative versions. (I discuss the reasons for this in Chapter 1.) Changes of detail or emphasis from one version to another made it possible to shift and even reverse the point of a tale. The classical poets could and did make some rather controversial points by introducing the issues of their own times into their treatments of ancient stories. Vase paintings depict otherwise unknown versions, or conflations of known versions. Thus the modern rewriting of myths is a continuation of ancient practice.

10

The doubleness of myth – its combination of strangeness and familiarity – allows it to be used either to shore up traditional values or to contest them in an acceptable way. Sometimes this is done consciously, as when a conservative thinker such as William Bennett (the American Secretary of Education under Ronald Reagan) includes myths in his *Book of Virtues* for family reading,[2] or when a feminist publishes a *Book of Goddesses* emphasizing the independence and benevolence of these powerful female figures.[3] More often, I think, the author of a retelling has no conscious ideological message. Yet this does not mean that such a work has no ideological implications or effects. Classical myths carry no overt religious or political messages that could offend the citizens of an increasingly secular and 'globalized' society. Yet they retain a cultural prestige derived from their connection to the Greek and Roman cultures and to the Western literary and artistic canon. At the same time, the basic plots of the stories reflect a hierarchical world order that still matches most people's experience of work, school, and family life. Thus the myths do not conflict with, and may reinforce, the process of socialization into economic and gender systems still dominated by Western models.

This effect is not inevitable, however. Those who live within the same system do not all see it from the same angle. Not only authors but audiences occupy different positions within the system, and these differences can shape the ways a story is told or 'read'. Here again the example of the ancient versions can illuminate our situation. Although most were composed by and for elite males, ancient versions belonged to diverse types or *genres* of literature, and there is increasing recognition that women and lower-class men could be included in the intended audiences of some of these genres. Even within the male elite there could be strong disagreements and 'subversive' viewpoints. So even the ancient versions do not present a monolithic endorsement of the prevailing ideologies of their times. *A fortiori*, the self-consciously pluralistic culture of our time should make room for retellings of the myths from a wide range of perspectives, including some with the potential to unsettle the hierarchies that the stories assume.

Even among the most radical critics of ideology, however, there

11

are few who would argue that human beings can do without it altogether. In this apparent human need I see a further reason for the persistence of myth. We seem to need stories to position ourselves in the world – to develop a sense of identity. This need is especially strong among children and adolescents, but we never outgrow it. Myths are traditional stories that come to us with the implicit endorsement of time and of a cultural community. They offer us a sense of connection to that community and to those we think of as our ancestors. In this perspective it may not be paradoxical after all that a time of rapid cultural change should foster a revival of interest in mythology. Like the Greek god Proteus, a myth can assume an indefinite series of different forms and still be perceived as one entity. This may be a delusion, but it need not be a pernicious one if by its reassurance of continuity it can promote creative change.

Gender is a central component of identity. So it is no wonder that gender differences have been emphasized in most versions of the myths, ancient and modern. It may seem to some observers that a modern preoccupation with gender *conflict*, growing out of women's movements for social and political rights, has distorted our view of the ancient myths by importing distinctively modern concerns into our readings of them. But a hard, honest look at the ancient texts reveals an equal preoccupation with gender conflict. In these stories wives kill husbands (sometimes en masse!), mothers kill sons, and fathers sacrifice daughters with distressing regularity. The specific forms and causes of gender conflict in our age are clearly different from those in ancient Greece and Rome, but there can be no doubt that such conflict existed then as now. Its acuteness, as reflected in the myths, may even have been precipitated by shifts in the ancient gender systems, which we can only partially recover from the evidence that has survived.

The twentieth century witnessed an intense interest in the interpretation of mythology, encompassing many approaches. Most of these were academic in origin, but all have reached the popular press and some have inspired fervent interest in the 'lay' public. I have organized this book as a survey and critique of some of the most prominent approaches, taking care to include 'popularizing' works whose wide appeal testifies that they have struck a chord beyond the academic community. My focus throughout is on the ways in which the various approaches have dealt – or failed to deal – with the relationship between myths and gender systems. A vast amount of work has already been done on this topic, but it tends to be presented in journal articles and works of specialized scholarship. I am deeply indebted to those who have preceded me in the field and whose works are cited in the chapters that follow; I could not have found space for all of them even in a much longer work. My aim in this volume is to synthesize some of this pioneering work and link it to issues in the culture at large.

In keeping with a Western intellectual tradition that has only recently begun to change, most established systems of myth interpretation are founded on the work of 'great men': Freud, Jung, Eliade, Lévi-Strauss. Because this book is a reflection on the 'state of the art' – an overview and critique of *existing* systems – a disproportionate amount of it will be devoted to the work of these men. It would have been possible to write an account of myth interpretation based entirely on feminist theory, but for a classicist, even a feminist classicist, this would have been a much more difficult task. I certainly do not mean to give the impression that feminist thought is merely reactive, a kind of supplement to the concerns of male scholars. Rather, I hope to demonstrate that neglect (however unconscious) of gender systems has left serious flaws in most current approaches.

Myth interpretation is often theoretical or at least grounded in theory. By explaining basic concepts and defining terminology I have tried to make the various theories comprehensible to the educated but nonspecialist reader. At the same time I have used many concrete examples from the myths to clarify the stakes of interpretation. For variety's sake, rather than illustrate the differences between approaches by applying each in turn to the same myth, I have used different myths in each chapter . Considerations of length prevent me from summarizing some of the better-known myths. The reader is encouraged to consult a dictionary of mythology for this basic information. A few of my examples are drawn not from ancient versions but from modern retellings or from frankly modern fictions with some connection of plot or theme to the classical myths. Works of this kind, some of which are hugely popular, can help us gauge both the connections and the gaps between the roles myths have played in ancient gender systems and in our own. Insofar as myths participate in, reinforce, and challenge gender ideologies, they have influence in the 'real world'. I have tried never to lose sight of this fact.

1

Myth and Gender Systems

Versions, modern and ancient

In what forms do we tend to encounter classical myths today?[1] Suppose a curious American eighteen-year-old (whom we'll call Sara) is intrigued by the tale of Demeter and Persephone as she sees it re-enacted in 'The Other Side', an episode of the television series *Hercules: The Legendary Journeys*.[2] Hades, king of the underworld, kidnaps Persephone, daughter of the goddess Demeter. The anxious mother appeals to Hercules for help, and when he refuses to interfere in a quarrel between gods Demeter unleashes storms of rain, sleet and snow to make him change his mind. Going below, he finds Persephone half in love with her captor and persuades her to leave only by describing the devastation Demeter is causing in her absence. But Hades is unwilling to let her go and Hercules must defeat him in a duel – before negotiating a compromise by which Persephone will spend six months of the year with her mother and six with Hades.

If Sara looks around for other versions of this myth, what is she likely to find?

First she remembers seeing Edith Hamilton's *Mythology* on her parents' shelf of old college texts. Here she finds a very different story from the one told in the TV show, though the plot is recognizable.[3] Hercules is nowhere to be found. The central character is Demeter, and there is a long subplot about her failed attempt to adopt a human baby – a little boy. Persephone is a very reluctant bride, and the lengthy negotiations needed to end the famine on earth are carried on between Zeus and Demeter, with many divine intermediaries. Demeter is finally persuaded to accept the compromise by 'Rhea, the oldest of the gods', who is identified as Zeus' mother. The story is framed by an essay in which Hamilton explains that Demeter and Dionysus were 'altogether different' from the rest of the Greek gods in the degree of their concern for human beings. Demeter in particular was 'always kind'; 'she was sorry for the desolation she had brought about' and compensated humanity by teaching them to sow grain and celebrate her secret rites.

At the local public library, Sara finds *Bulfinch's Mythology: The Age of Fable*.[4] All the names of the main characters have changed (to Latin, as Bulfinch explains in his introduction), and the story has some curious new details: Hades (now called Pluto) falls in love with Persephone (now Proserpine) when he is struck by one of Cupid's arrows. The family whose baby Demeter/Ceres adopts is poor, and the father plays a more prominent role in the story. Two water nymphs, Cyane and Arethusa, give Ceres the information she got from the Sun (Greek *Helios*) in Hamilton's version; when she learns where her daughter is, she goes straight to Zeus/Jupiter and 'implores' him to intervene.

At a used-book sale, Sara picks up a paperback from the 1960s called *The Greek Gods* by Evslin, Evslin, and Hoopes.[5] In the chapter on Demeter, she finds yet another version of the story, in which Persephone is described as 'a flower child' whose job is to invent and name new kinds of flowers. The relationship between Hades and Persephone is straight out of a Harlequin or Mills and Boon romance:

> Although she never forgot how he had frightened her ... , she admired the lofty set of his black-robed figure, the majestic shoulders, the great impatient hands, and his gloomy black eyes. But she knew that part of her power over him was disdain, and so kept flouting and abusing him ... (27)

It is not Hades who tempts her to eat the pomegranate seeds, but a strange boy, newly arrived in the underworld after being turned into a lizard by Demeter for laughing at her in her grief.

Sara's older brother, visiting for the holidays, shows her a graphic novel (for 'mature readers') he acquired in high school, in which the story of Demeter and Persephone is set in fifth-century Athens with a cast of supporting characters led by the philosopher Epicurus and including Plato, Aristotle, and a bratty little boy named Alexander (someday to be known as 'the Great').[6] Here Demeter is a gigantic, voluptuous nude towering over the human characters; even her daughter is afraid of her, and has allowed 'Hadespoo' to stage the abduction to get around 'Mummy's' objections to their marriage. The role of negotiator is taken by Epicurus, who secretly advises Persephone to eat the seeds so Demeter will be forced to compromise. In fact, the whole episode of the 'visit to Hades' is framed by Epicurus' attempts to make sense of a world that seems intractable to his philosophical ideals of logic and moderation.

Sara's little niece comes to visit her, bringing a children's version of the myth called *The Pomegranate Seeds* by Laura Geringer.[7] The story is close to that in the Evslin version, but with a tone more appropriate to a children's book. An interesting 'Author's Note' informs the reader that this version 'is inspired by Nathaniel Hawthorne's "Pomegranate Seeds," published in *Tanglewood Tales* in 1853, which emphasizes the coming-of-age theme and underplays Persephone's kidnapping'. The author adds, 'My Persephone is a more modern and outspoken girl than Hawthorne's. And like a present-day working mother, Demeter, though conflicted about leaving her daughter, must tend to her job.' Sara finds Hawthorne's version at the library (in a 1968 edition)[8] and, given its age, is struck more by the similarities than by the differences between it and Geringer's. In neither does there seem to be anything sexual about the relationship between Hades and Persephone; he is her lonely old uncle, who just wants 'a merry little maid' ('a lively little girl' in Geringer) to keep him company in his gloomy kingdom. On her side, Persephone develops an affection for him that makes her willing to accept her six months in the underworld (reduced to three in Geringer). Zeus has disappeared from the story, so that there is neither confrontation nor negotiation between him and Demeter.

Starting college in the fall, Sara enrolls in a mythology course and decides to ask her teacher for help in sorting out all these versions. The teacher refers her to recent translations of two ancient texts: the *Homeric Hymn to Demeter* and the second half of Book 5 of Ovid's *Metamorphoses*.[9] In these two very different works, Sara recognizes

17

most, but not all, of the details that appear in various combinations in the versions she had found on her own. The ancient works, however – one Greek and the other Latin – are themselves separated by at least six hundred years, a far greater gap even than that between Hawthorne and Geringer. Sara is surprised to find that in the *Homeric Hymn* – by far the oldest available version of this myth – Demeter is portrayed as more powerful than in most subsequent versions. Motivated by anger as much as by grief, she is capable of destroying the human race and wiping out the privileges of the gods by 'hiding' the seed and not letting it grow. Far from appealing to Zeus for help, she ignores a whole string of his emissaries – who offer her gifts and 'whatever honours she would choose among the immortals' – until he himself capitulates and sends the messenger god Hermes to bring back Persephone. The real negotiator in this version, though, is the goddess Rhea, who by the logic of the story seems to be chosen because she is *Demeter's* mother (though she is Zeus' as well): she calls Demeter 'child', and their meeting is a joyful one like that of Demeter and Persephone (lines 458-60). While the goddesses must accept the permanence of Persephone's marriage and Hades is repeatedly described as a worthy match for her, there is no attempt to justify his abduction of her or to portray any emotional ties between husband and wife.

In Ovid's version, despite the fact that Dis (the Roman name for Hades – Pluto is actually another Greek name) is smitten with desire for Proserpina, there is still no mutual affection, and the theme of rape is reinforced by a long digression in which the nymph Arethusa describes her own attempted rape by the river Alpheus. Arethusa's ultimate escape, like that of the better-known Daphne when pursued by Apollo, requires her transformation into something non-human – in her case, a spring. In fact, no fewer than seven such transformations are described or alluded to in this retelling of the myth, which is subordinated to the larger themes and narrative framework of Ovid's *Metamorphoses*. Not only does Ceres change the boy who laughs at her into a lizard, but the underworld spirit who reports that Proserpina has eaten the pomegranate seeds is turned into a screech-owl by Proserpina herself. The story as a whole is presented as the Muse Calliope's entry in a singing contest, one of those fatal contests in which mortals dare to rival gods. Predictably, the mortals, daughters of Pierus, lose and are changed to magpies for their arrogance. While Ovid clearly relishes these transformations as displays of his own virtuosic performance as a poet, he also explores what we would call their psychological dimension. Thus he dwells on the appropriateness of the new form a character assumes, and on the trauma of being 'taken away from oneself' (*sibi ablatus*, line 546). It is not surprising, given this latter focus, that so many of the metamorphoses should result from rapes or attempted rapes.

I have drawn out this series of examples to underline a number of points about the myths in both their ancient and modern versions. The most obvious of these points – that the myths have continued to attract tellers and audiences for close to three thousand years – is also in a way the most puzzling, since it should be clear from my brief survey that the stories change radically from one version to the next, even when the versions are contemporary with one another. Retellers ancient and modern have freely altered the motives of the characters, the sequence of narrative events, and the point(s) of view from which they are told. What is more, these narrative building blocks, themselves so variable, have been used to evoke a vast range of themes: the love of mother and daughter, to be sure, but also the daughter's fear of the mother and manipulation of the husband, the husband's desire for a wife, even the poet's (and humorist's) virtuosity and the philosopher's desire to make sense of 'illogical' reality. What, then, is the myth of Demeter and Persephone 'about'? The answer must be that it has an enormous range of potential meanings, only some of which have yet been tapped.

If a myth is so variable, does it make sense even to call it 'a' myth? Does a myth exist as something more than, or other than, a series of discrete texts and images? Ordinary language usage would suggest that it does: we speak routinely of 'the myth of Demeter and Persephone'. All that *survives* from the ancient world is a congeries of texts and visual images, some datable, some not. But there must have been innumerable versions of these same stories – oral performances and informal retellings as well as texts and works of art – that have been lost. And most classical myths continued to be

19

retold long after the ancient societies had passed away; many of them, as the children's books and television series mentioned above make clear, are still being retold today. Should these facts have any influence on the way we interpret the myths?

Most of the lost versions are irrevocably lost, though a few may yet be retrieved from the earth by archaeologists. But the fact that they existed is not a negligible one. For a myth is not just any fiction. To become a myth, a story must have been retold often enough to become familiar to many, if not most, members of a community over several generations; and as a result, it carries a certain authority – if not that of religious tradition, at least that of survival and of peer acceptance. It cannot be truly marginal and still be considered a myth.

At the same time, the great differences among surviving versions of certain classical myths make us aware that poets and artists had great license to reimagine and reinterpret them. The religions of Greece and Rome resembled each other, and differed from the monotheistic faiths of more recent times, in emphasizing practice over belief. What mattered was what one did in honour of the gods, not what one believed about them. As long as the traditional festivals were observed and the prescribed offerings made in the prescribed ways, it was thought that the gods would be satisfied. So there was no formal canon of scripture, no catechism, no schools of theology. To some extent, the differences among mythic variants are due to changes in the Greek and Roman cultures over time; this is clear when we compare Aeschylus' view of Prometheus with Hesiod's, or Seneca's Medea with Euripides'. And some differences clearly reflect the attitudes of individual artists, as we can see by observing the distinctive 'Ovidian' or 'Senecan' or 'Euripidean' features of those authors' retellings.

What difference does it make that nearly all surviving ancient versions of the myths are by male authors? Undeniably a male poet is capable of portraying vivid female characters, or making one the protagonist of a work, or putting words in her mouth that express attitudes different from those the male characters say she should have. (Think of Aeschylus' Clytemnestra, or of almost any Euripidean heroine.) From the literature of subsequent eras, we know that women and men can portray one another with realism and sensitivity. When virtually *all* our testimony comes from men, however, we must ask if we are missing something important – especially when a culture, like that of ancient Greece, kept men and women apart for many activities. One thing we may be missing, to judge from cross-cultural comparisons, is a body of folklore, including versions of myths, produced by women for women. That such tales exist in many cultures has been realized only since women began doing anthropological fieldwork: they gained access to women's traditions that were closed to their male counterparts, and even to men within the culture under study. (See Chapter 2 for an example from India.) The meagre surviving fragments of Greek women's poetry, especially that of Sappho, give us tantalizing glimpses of this kind of 'women's world'. Unfortunately for my purposes, most of the little writing by women that survives is lyric rather than narrative poetry, with few clear references to mythic material. In the late twentieth century, women writers have self-consciously sought to remedy this gap in the classical tradition by retelling the myths from the points of view of the female characters.[10] The range of genres and styles in which these retellings have appeared – from the poetry of Margaret Atwood and Carol Ann Duffy to the stories of Marina Warner, the novels of Marion Zimmer Bradley, and the television serial *Xena, Warrior Princess* – suggests that the effort to reclaim a distinctive 'women's classical tradition' appeals to many women and at least some men at the turn of the millennium.[11]

An interesting case can be made for the possibility that the *Homeric Hymn to Demeter*, or the poem on which it is based, may be female-authored. Ann Suter believes that the *Hymn* consists of two parts: a 'core story' of Persephone's abduction, which can be read as a psychological 'coming of age narrative', and an 'Olympian frame' asserting that the abduction was arranged between Zeus and Hades.[12] In Suter's reading, Persephone's interest in the narcissus is symbolic of her readiness for, and interest in, adult sexuality; it is her reaching to pick it that precipitates the action of the core story. To Demeter, she describes her eating of the pomegranate seed as forced on her, but this can be seen as 'a prototypical young girl's story to

21

her mother', edited to placate Demeter. While the Olympian frame is clearly 'in the male voice', affirming patriarchal control of events,

> the core story just as clearly is in the female voice: women are the active subjects as well as objects; women control events; relationships are adjusted on the basis of understanding, accommodation, sharing, rather than hierarchization; the predominant motivation for action is love, not power; the matrilineal line is emphasized.

Suter argues that the *Hymn* was composed as an *aition* (account of origin) not only of the Eleusinian Mysteries but of the women's festival called the Thesmophoria, where it may have been performed 'by a woman, for women'.

Suter's balanced discussion acknowledges that women can speak in 'the male voice', adopting, or at least mouthing, patriarchal values; and she makes the important point that 'male' or 'female', as descriptions of the 'voice' of a poem, should not be equated with the biological sex of the author. We know that Greek women composed lyric poetry of the highest quality and that some composed in hexameters, the metre of epic; is it impossible that some of them should have mastered the compositional technique of 'Homeric' verse, in which the *Hymn to Demeter* was cast? We tend to assume that women were barred from the traditional apprenticeship by which male bards learned their art, but a remarkable instance of women performing oral epic has recently been reported from nineteenth and twentieth century Dalmatia.[13] Very little of their material has yet been published. Given the short time that scholarship has concerned itself with women's traditions, it is too early to foreclose the possibilities of women's participation in art forms we tend to think of as masculine.

Gender systems

I chose to begin with the myth of Demeter because the variety of existing versions makes especially clear the complex relationships

22

between myths and systems of gender relationships in both the ancient and the modern world. Hard as we may try, we can never completely divorce ourselves from the nexus of gendered meanings and practices in our own world, which for convenience I will call our 'gender system'.[14] In their modern, adapted versions, the classical myths are 'naturalized' into our gender system – for instance, by making Hades and Persephone 'fall in love' with each other; in their ancient versions, the myths reflect the ancient systems in and for which they were produced – for instance, by emphasizing Zeus' attempt to arrange a marriage for his daughter. There are enough similarities between the ancient and modern systems to make the ancient versions intelligible to us, but many of their details are puzzling until we place them back into their ancient contexts.

Let me begin by outlining some of the most salient features of the Greek and Roman gender systems and noting both similarities and differences between these systems and our own. In such a survey oversimplification is inevitable, since every gender system has many components whose interrelationships evolve over time. Keep in mind, then, that these are only the broad outlines; some of the nuances and exceptions will be filled in by later chapters.[15] Because this book is concerned with myths, I omit other systems of thought such as medicine and philosophy, which were undeniable elements of these gender systems but which have complexities of their own requiring fuller treatment than I can give them here. Myth has an especially complex relationship to religion; the gods, to cite only one difficulty, could be understood very differently and could play very different roles in myth and in cult.

I illustrate the survey by relating details of the gender systems to the versions of the Demeter myth I have just outlined. Some essential elements of the gender systems have no parallels in this myth but are included in the survey because of their intrinsic importance. Since the gods of classical myth were humans writ large, sometimes subject to the limitations of human existence and sometimes escaping these limits in spectacular ways,[16] their stories illustrate the cultures that produced them by contrast as well as by direct reflection. This survey is an introduction, then, to the dialectical relationship between myths and reality that makes myths 'good to think with'.

Our view of the Greek gender system has long been skewed by the fact that a disproportionate amount of the surviving evidence comes from the city of Athens in the 'classical' era, i.e. the fifth and fourth centuries BCE. Paradoxically, the first Greek democracy put more limitations on its women's activities than did some other city-states, to judge by the fragmentary evidence that survives from elsewhere. Yet throughout Greece in the so-called 'archaic' and 'classical' periods, most women were economically and legally dependent on men, who held all political authority and handled most economic transactions. (Sparta, where women could inherit property, may have been an exception to the latter rule.) This situation is clearly reflected in the *Hymn to Demeter*, a product of the early 'archaic' period (*c.* 600 BCE): the women of Eleusis must turn to their men to satisfy Demeter's demand that a temple be built in her honour. In legal transactions, a woman was never treated as an adult: throughout her life she needed a male 'master' (*kyrios,* often translated 'guardian'), usually a father, husband, or son, to act on her behalf. Demeter is clearly exempt from this requirement because she is a goddess, and she is outraged when Zeus – who is the father of her child, but not her husband – behaves as though he alone had authority over Persephone. Although the divine hierarchy included elements of gender hierarchy, the most powerful goddesses were thought to escape some of its provisions. At her marriage, a woman received from her father a dowry that was intended for her support and that had to be returned with her if she were divorced. Daughters were sometimes portrayed as liabilities because they would inevitably leave their birth families, taking valuable property with them. The *Hymn to Demeter* omits the mundane details of the dowry[17] but suggests that daughters may have been more highly valued – and their departure at marriage more keenly regretted – by mothers than by fathers.

Girls were married in their early teens to men who were normally at least ten years older than they. This is reflected in the age difference between Persephone and Hades, who is her uncle. (Nieces were married to paternal uncles with some frequency, since this kept their dowries in the family.) The marriage ceremony, which required no verbal consent from the bride, consisted principally of a procession from the bride's house to the groom's as she was transferred from her family to his. Some pictures on Greek wedding vases, in which bride and groom ride in a chariot or the groom leads the bride by the wrist while her mother carries a torch in the procession, have been interpreted as evoking details of Persephone's abduction and Demeter's torchlight search for her (most weddings took place at night).[18] Girls who died before marriage were referred to as 'brides of Hades'. Although women were raised to expect this radical transition in their lives, it must have been difficult and even traumatic for some, who may have experienced it as a rape – especially if the groom were unknown to them, as was often the case. Even the fact that eating seeds binds Persephone to Hades had an echo in the Greek wedding, since the bride ate a quince or seedcake in her new home, presumably to symbolize the prospect of her fertility.

Virtually all people, men and women, were married for some part of their lives, and were expected to produce children, especially sons to inherit the father's property and perpetuate the 'family cult', i.e. the offerings made to dead members of the (father's) family. Because the gods are immortal they do not need to replace themselves by reproduction, yet because they are anthropomorphic they do so, with sometimes problematic consequences (see Chapter 2). Hades and Persephone are unique among divine couples in failing to produce a child (though in some unusual versions of the myth they do). A puzzling detail of the *Hymn* is Demeter's attempt to adopt a human boy. On one level he is clearly a replacement for her lost daughter, but the difference of sex suggests that a son, who cannot be taken away and who will enjoy the privileges of masculinity, is a 'safe' replacement, even a potential champion for Demeter in her opposition to Zeus.

Most forms of work were gender-specific, with outdoor tasks – most agricultural work, commerce, warfare, and government – assigned to males and indoor tasks – spinning, weaving, food preparation and storage, the care of children and the sick – to females. In households that could afford slaves, much of the work

25

was done by them and supervised by the mistress of the house – the wife or mother of the owner. For slaves too, work was largely gender-specific. The women of a household, slave and free, thus spent much of their time together and apart from the men; husbands and wives did not even dine together, at least when guests were present. This gender segregation is reflected throughout the *Hymn*: Persephone is gathering flowers with other goddesses when she is abducted; in her mortal disguise, Demeter has contact only with the female members of the household she visits; and while Zeus employs the male Hermes as messenger to Hades, he sends the goddess Iris and later Demeter's (and his own) mother Rhea as envoys to Demeter.

Religious activities, like work, were often, though not always, segregated by gender. Although male and female deities were worshipped by both sexes, a large number of cults and cult activities were gender-specific. The Eleusinian Mysteries, whose foundation is described at the end of the *Hymn*, were open to women and men alike and presided over by priests and priestesses who were thought to be descendants of the Eleusinian families named in the *Hymn*. Other rites of Demeter, however, including the Thesmophoria, which have also been linked to the *Hymn*, were celebrated by women only. At the Thesmophoria the fertility of grain and the fertility of women were symbolically linked. The metaphor of woman as the 'ground' in which the man's seed is 'planted' became almost a cliché of Greek poetry – though the actual extent of the woman's contribution to her child's heredity was a subject of constant debate in medicine and philosophy.

As might be expected, there are important aspects of the gender system that are not reflected in the *Hymn to Demeter*. Since these are reflected in other myths, I briefly sketch them here. A double standard of sexual conduct, which permitted some kinds of extramarital sex to men but not to women, led to the division of free women into two basic classes, those who were 'respectable', i.e., marriageable, and those who were not. Slaves, both women and men, were *ipso facto* ineligible for legal marriage and sexually available to their masters. (The existence of slavery is at least alluded to in the *Hymn* when Demeter tells Metaneira's daughters that she has escaped from pirates who wanted to sell her.) Sexual relations between males were permitted and perhaps customary in certain highly specific circumstances – between an older *erastês* ('lover') and a pubescent *erômenos* ('beloved') to whom he acted as both lover and mentor for a limited time. Analogous relationships between women are suggested by some lyric poetry[19] and in Plutarch's *Life of Lycurgus* (18).

The Roman gender system was similar to the Greek in many ways but had its own distinctive features. On the one hand, the power of the father over his family (*patria potestas*) was even greater, at least in theory: not even a son achieved legal adulthood or the right to own property in his own name until he was 'emancipated' by the death of his father. All children bore the father's name (which was also the family name, the *nomen*), in a masculine form for boys and a feminine form for girls. Yet boys were given individual first names (*praenomina*), while girls were not.

On the other hand, Roman women – at least those of the late Republic and early Empire, when most of the mythic texts I will discuss were written – enjoyed greater social freedom than was the norm for Athenian women. While most types of work were still gender-specific and therefore segregated, women spent more time socializing with the men of their own households and did not risk a reputation for unchastity by dining with or speaking to men who were not their relatives. As a result, they could and did lobby for political programmes – usually, to be sure, those of their husbands or brothers. On occasion, they even staged public demonstrations to support or oppose specific legislation. The unofficial power of a few individual women – members of the imperial family – was greatly enhanced by the change in the Roman system of government from republic to autocracy. Even the republic, however, was an aristocratic system in which women were valued as the transmitters of bloodlines. It has been argued that Roman fathers saw daughters, like sons, as perpetuating their personal traits and abilities, and that women so valued were empowered to exercise these abilities themselves – sometimes even in the public sphere.[20]

Some of these distinctive features of the Roman system may be reflected in the version of the Demeter myth told by Ovid. His Ceres still turns to other females for help initially, but upon learning her daughter's fate she confronts Jupiter directly and appeals to his paternal feelings: 'If you have no regard for the mother, at least let the daughter touch her father's heart' (5.515-16).[21] Surprisingly, the abduction is not arranged between Jupiter and Dis (Pluto) but instigated by Cupid at the command of his mother Venus. Her motive is to extend her own power (*imperium*) as goddess of desire by bringing Dis' kingdom under her yoke and preventing Proserpina from remaining a virgin like Minerva/Athena and Diana/Artemis. Her language is clearly meant to suggest Roman imperial ambitions, but these are presented as a female's bid for power over her peers within the ruling elite.

The Romans recognized two forms of marriage that had different implications for the woman involved. If she was married 'with *manus*' (*cum manu*), her husband became her legal guardian and she became a member of his family. If married 'without *manus*' (*sine manu*), however, she remained a member of her birth family and one of its members – such as her father or brother – served as her guardian. Since Roman women could inherit property, the choice of a form of marriage dictated whose heirs they would be, their husband's or their father's. A father who retained his authority over a married daughter might seek to dissolve her marriage and arrange a new one to suit his own political or economic purposes. Yet a woman whose guardian was not her husband also had more leverage in disputes with the husband and could obtain a divorce more easily. Divorce among the elite became increasingly common in the late republic for both these reasons: fathers using it to shift political alliances and wives to withdraw from marriages in which they were unhappy. Conservative orators railed against the spread of marriage 'without *manus*' on the grounds that it fostered divorce and moral laxity – which, by implication, resulted when women were allowed greater independence from their husbands' control. In practice, the guardian's power was also eroded over time until in the case of elite women, at least, it became largely *pro forma*.

Although none of this background surfaces in Ovid's version, it provides a context in which many of his details make sense. Ceres addresses Jupiter in language that would suit a divorced wife addressing her former husband: 'Let not your care for [Proserpina] be less because I am her mother' (5.516-17). Yet she sounds self-assured in her position and anything but apologetic. In urging him to dissolve Proserpina's marriage, she argues that Dis is a 'robber' and thus morally unfit – the only grounds on which a Roman woman could legally reject the groom her father proposed. Jupiter reminds Ceres that Dis is his brother, yet he is willing to let her have her way; the outcome is determined by 'the fates', who rule that because she has eaten in the underworld Proserpina must return to it periodically.

Another feature of Ovid's version is the emphasis on rape as seen from the woman's perspective. The water nymph Cyane tries to block Dis' chariot on the grounds that a woman should be 'wooed' (or 'asked'), not raped. When Dis evades her, she literally dissolves in tears so that she cannot speak when Ceres comes in search of her daughter. The nymph Arethusa, who does give her the information, was herself the victim of attempted rape, which she avoided only by praying to the virgin goddess Diana, who transformed her into a spring. Like many of the rapes described by Ovid this one seems designed to appeal to at least two audiences: the description of the naked, beautiful, vulnerable nymph can be read as titillating to a voyeuristic male audience, while her description of her own terror and her empathy with the fear of Proserpina (5.506) emphasize the woman's side of the story.

It is sometimes assumed that 'Roman mythology' is merely Greek mythology with Roman names. This is a serious misunderstanding. Although the Romans did borrow great numbers of Greek myths, they adapted them to their own cultural situation in ways both obvious and subtle. They also had stories of their own about the early history of Rome that – whatever their connection to 'history' as we define it – served many of the functions of myth. As in the Greek stories about mortal women, there is a tendency to classify women characters as good or bad on the basis of their loyalty or disloyalty to male kin. Yet some of the women in Roman legend are exemplary for their public, if not political, roles: the Sabine women venture onto the battlefield to make peace between their fathers and their husbands, while the mother of Coriolanus puts loyalty to Rome above loyalty to her son and is able to dissuade him from attacking his city.

At first glance, the contrasts between these gender systems and our own seem overwhelming, especially since the recent changes brought about by women's movements for civil and social equity. At least in law, women in Western Europe and North America have full civil rights and can serve in any governmental office. Girls and boys usually attend the same schools and study the same subjects. Women own and manage their own property and have gained access to most forms of employment, including the professions that require advanced education. As a result, women need not be financially dependent on men. Marriage is a personal choice for both parties; divorce and cohabitation without marriage are common and socially acceptable. It is even acceptable for women living alone to bear or adopt children, and long-term unions between two men or two women are gaining social acceptability if not legal recognition. In marriage and other long-term sexual relationships there is an ideal of friendship and mutual desire between the partners. Thus all the modern retellings of the Demeter myth include some mutual attachment between Hades and Persephone, either predating the abduction or developing gradually after it.

But there are discrepancies between legal possibilities and the actual state of affairs: thus in the United States in the year 2000, although women had had the right to vote since 1920, only one woman in the history of the country had served as Attorney General, one as Secretary of State, and a total of 22 as members of presidential cabinets (4.5% of 487). Two had served as Supreme Court justices; none had been elected President or Vice-President, and only one had ever been nominated for Vice-President by a major political party. Nine out of 100 Senators and 56 of 435 Representatives in the Congress were women.[22] Women are still disproportionately employed in lower-wage jobs and earn on average 76 cents for every dollar earned by men. Thus within heterosexual couples the woman is likely to be earning less than the man and to be financially dependent on him to some extent. Women have made rapid strides in the professions, especially medicine and law, but administrators at the highest levels are disproportionately male. So the gender hierarchy that prevailed in the ancient cultures and that was reflected in their myths is still largely intact. It makes sense to a modern audience that Demeter and Persephone have less authority than the male gods and must use subversive tactics such as a strike or passive resistance to get their way. Paradoxically, while many modern versions omit Zeus, some of them introduce a new male character – Hercules or Epicurus, in the versions described above – to resolve the crisis, either by defeating Hades in a duel or by negotiating a 'settlement' between Demeter and Hades.

Another element of the ancient gender systems that survives today is the expectation that a woman will take primary responsibility for the running of a household and that a mother of children will provide or arrange for most of their care. If, as in the United States, there is no governmental support for day care, women who work outside the home must cobble together private solutions, most of which involve hiring other women as caregivers. Given this situation, it is surprising that few modern versions of the Demeter myth even include the episode in which the disguised Demeter is hired to care for a human baby. This may simply be because most modern versions are based on Ovid's, which omits the episode. Yet to include it would be to raise in a more acute form the issue of women's ambivalence and guilt about leaving their children with other women. The modern versions may be expressing this guilt more tacitly by devoting more space than the ancient ones to the emotional connection between mother and daughter. Demeter's mothering role is even explicitly linked to her responsibility for the growth of grain and, by extension, her 'motherly' care for all humanity. Modern interpreters feel obliged to explain that she was very sorry for the suffering she caused the human race and that she made it up to them by teaching them the Mysteries and the principles of agriculture. Sometimes the sterility of the earth during Persephone's absence is described as a sympathetic reaction to Demeter's grief; in Geraldine McCaughrean's version, 'the trees wept with her, shedding their leaves'.[23]

Some modern versions also portray Demeter as anxious about her daughter even before the abduction because she is obliged to leave her alone. This clearly reflects the working mother's concern for the safety of her children, as well as the heightened awareness of sexual abuse and rape as real and widespread dangers. Violence against women and even sexual harrassment are illegal in America at the turn of the century but both are still epidemic. The desire to shelter children from this reality may account for the desexualized versions of the myth designed for children, in which Hades plays the lonely old uncle who needs the company of his little niece to cheer him up.

As in the ancient cultures, women today are divided by class and privilege, and the divisions often fall along ethnic lines (as in Greece and Rome most slaves were prisoners of war or their descendants). Now as then, the stories that receive widest distribution tend to focus on characters who are at least moderately privileged, and to be told from their point of view. Yet even in ancient Greece and Rome the perspectives of lower-class characters were sometimes included.[24] One not uncommon type of story featured a god who assumed a human – even a lower-class – disguise to test the hospitality of mortals. Some interpreters of the Demeter story have argued that her special concern for mortals, expressed in her gift of the Mysteries that mitigated the fear of death, should be linked to her experience of the human condition as grieving mother and as servant/nursemaid in a human household.[25] Of course, a temporary identification with a person of lower status is not likely to unsettle one's relation to the social hierarchy in any profound way, and may even reinforce it by suggesting that charity to the 'unfortunate' is all that is required. Yet the story of Demeter also suggests a commensurability of female experience across class divisions, including the great divide between the 'class' of gods and all classes of mortals.

To me, the most striking effect of comparing a range of ancient and modern versions of the Demeter myth is the revelation that the oldest surviving version, that of the *Homeric Hymn*, gives Demeter the strongest role in the story's outcome and makes her anger as important as her grief. Although her resistance to Zeus may be passive by comparison to her quarrel with him in Ovid, she demonstrates in a spectacular way that he cannot do without her and that her approval should therefore be sought in decisions that affect her. The paradox that Demeter is strongest in the oldest surviving version is explained by some scholars as reflecting an actual loss of status for women at some point in prehistory. (The evidence for this will be examined in Chapter 4.) Yet the same paradox should caution us against assuming that women in what we consider oppressively patriarchal systems are unconscious of their oppression and unable to protest against it.

As in antiquity, the stories we tell ourselves today – or read to ourselves, or 'consume' by watching television or video – bear a complicated relation to our gender system. They may sustain it by assuring us that it is good, or getting better. They may hold out visions of radical or incremental change in various utopian futures, or conjure up dystopias in which the rights we enjoy are swept away. They may rewrite the past, as the *Xena: Warrior Princess* television series blends myth with history and with the conventions of modern fictional genres like soap opera and situation comedy. Already in antiquity there was a range of such *genres – types* of literary texts and/or performances – in which the myths were presented. Each genre had a distinctive audience for which it was shaped, although our knowledge of these audiences is limited by the gaps in our evidence; sometimes our only or primary evidence for the makeup of the audience is in the text itself. When classical myths or other traditional stories are retold or adapted to new media, they must be changed enough to appeal to the modern audience – as its tastes are understood by the producers of the media. While there is danger of corporate censorship as the media are owned by a shrinking number of huge conglomerates, the internet and affordable video cameras hold out the prospect that artists with small means will be able to reach a wide audience. 'Niche marketing', in the media as in other sectors of the economy, targets increasingly specific groups, some of which are all-male or all-female. Romances, tailored for women, are divided into multiple sub-genres according to the ages and tastes of the target audiences; mysteries, thrillers, and fantasy novels, which may be intended for male and/or female readers, are similarly diversified. Like the myths in their ancient contexts, all of these fictions participate in the gender system and sustain or challenge our individual senses of gender identity.

A gender system, then, is *both* a nexus of symbols and assumptions – expressed, among other ways, in stories – and a set of relationships in the 'real world'. We can live within such a system without being aware of it, just as we can speak our native languages without learning formal grammar, or retell a story without analysing its meaning. Even for those who are aware, elements of the system can remain below the threshold of consciousness most of the time. Sometimes this is due to a person's social status or role(s), which can blind her or him to whole areas of the system. But because it is 'the way things are', the gender system tends to become naturalized so that even its challengers act according to its prescriptions much of the time. This explains why 'consciousness-raising' – women's sharing of common experiences to reveal oppressive aspects of the system – has been such a powerful technique for feminists, but it also explains why consciousness-raising cannot be done once and for all.[26] It can be especially difficult to realize, and to *keep* in mind, that the gender system is part of a larger social reality in which social class, race, and membership in various subcultures affect the privileges and perceptions of every man and woman. We cannot assume that all women will share the same experiences, any more than we can make that assumption about all men. While all of us, male as well as female, can 'identify with' Demeter's loss of her daughter, different groups will see different things in her story and may react differently to it or identify more fully with Persephone, Hades, or some other character.

A gender system evolves over time. Sometimes the change is rapid, as it has been in our own time. Yet while some aspects of our system – such as the expectation that most women will work only in the home – have changed radically in recent years, other aspects – such as the expectation that most child care will be done by women – have not, and can even seem to be cast in stone. Such conservative elements may be shared by systems that are far removed from each other in time. This is one way to account for the enduring appeal of a myth like that of Demeter and Persephone: it continues to make sense to people of both sexes who have been reared primarily by their mothers.

In fact, feminists have argued that child-rearing arrangements are crucial to the 'reproduction' of the gender system, its transmission from generation to generation.[27] This is not just because mothers are our first teachers, but because the dependent state of infants makes the first years of life crucial to the development of identity, including gender identity. Psychologists believe that the conditions under which this development takes place leave an indelible imprint in the unconscious. Although psychologists tend to study the unconscious of the individual as shaped in the context of the family, their approach can also shed light on the unconscious dimension of larger social realities such as the gender system. And they can help us probe the deep connection between the stories we tell and the identities we forge for ourselves. In fact, modern psychology, beginning with Freud, has taken a keen interest in myths, both as evidence for the mental processes it studies and as phenomena to which its theories can be applied. I will argue in Chapter 5 that there is such a thing as a political or ideological unconscious, which is also reflected in myths.

I have noted that a given gender system evolves over time. Yet even when we attempt to 'freeze' the process for purposes of analysis, we find that such a view – called *synchronic* (that is, a view of data noted at the same point in time) – contains internal contradictions. For example, most systems contain contradictory stereotypes of each gender. In the Homeric epics, men are portrayed as the protectors of women, yet they capture the wives and daughters of other men and use them as slaves or concubines; indeed, the possession of such women is considered a mark of high honour. In the *Hymn to Demeter*, Zeus is Persephone's father and Hades her husband, two roles that ostensibly involve guardianship and protection. Yet Zeus permits, and Hades carries out, Persephone's forcible abduction. Other contradictions can be found between stereotypes and social practices or norms. Thus both Greek and Roman women were described as avid for wine and sex while men were thought to have greater control over their desires; yet men enjoyed much greater licence both in their use of wine and in their access to sexual gratification.[28]

The structuralist Claude Lévi-Strauss argued that the chief function of myths was to 'mediate' between contradictory elements in the ideology of a culture – to enable people to accept the contradictions by displacing them and providing a 'third term' that seemed to reconcile the apparent opposition. A god such as Dionysus, who combines attributes of both females and males and encourages his worshippers to assume temporarily the roles of the opposite gender,[29] might be seen as such a mediating figure in the opposition between the sexes that runs so deep in Greek culture.

A gender system, then, contains internal contradictions. At the same time, individuals and groups within a given society can disagree and argue openly about their gender system. Such disagreement is probably louder and more widespread today than it was in ancient times, but the *Hymn to Demeter* is clear proof that the ancient Greeks could imagine violent disagreement, with dramatic implications, about at least one aspect of their gender system, namely, the balance of power between father and mother in decisions about a daughter's marriage. As this example illustrates, differences of opinion are not purely idiosyncratic but often correspond with social roles and involve power imbalances or power struggles. The *Hymn* is today considered a particularly precious document because it emphasizes the viewpoints of a mother and daughter rather than those of the male figures in the story. Because nearly all the works to survive from antiquity were composed by men for largely male audiences, the viewpoints of male figures (characters and narrators) tend to predominate. Even in the work of male authors, however, we have evidence of disagreements over gender arrangements, not just between male and female characters but between male and male, female and female. In tragedy, female parts were played by men. Yet the tragedian Euripides created especially vivid female characters who speak explicitly of their hardships as women and of their disagreements with men. The chorus of his *Medea* (410-30) says that if women were poets, they would 'sing an answer' to the men who portray them as treacherous.

Yet even a work like the *Hymn to Demeter*, with its vivid portrayal of feminine protest against a father's unilateral decision, ends with the goddesses accepting the status quo, including the rule of Zeus and the marriage of Hades and Persephone. Does the myth actually make the status quo more palatable by providing an 'escape valve' for the protest? This raises the question of whether myths, and stories like them, necessarily help to shore up the gender system to which they belong. My answer is that it depends on the *version* and on the *audience*, since myths are never monolithic. As we have seen, they come in a variety of versions, representing a range of authors' perspectives. At the same time, each version can be received differently by different members of its audience. We can see this most clearly in the responses of our contemporaries. Thus Euripides, who produced some of the boldest variations on the myths, is read by most modern scholars as deliberately unsettling the norms of his society, including reverence for its gods; but even he has been read as affirming the gods' goodness and benevolence.[30] There must have been similar differences of opinion among the members of his original audience. Certainly there was disagreement about the value of his plays: he was repeatedly chosen as one of only three tragedians whose works were staged at civic expense, yet he very seldom won first or even second prize. That his ideas, and not merely his style, were debated can be seen from Aristophanes' comedy *Frogs*, where the god Dionysos is portrayed as having to choose a playwright – Aeschylus or Euripides – to bring back from the dead. While their styles are compared in detail, the god's decision ultimately hinges on the advice each poet has to offer the city. He chooses Aeschylus.

To summarize, then: a gender system is a nexus of ideas, images, and practices, functioning at a given time and place in the 'real world'. People can live within it and follow its rules while remaining largely unconscious of it. It changes over time, but it must be reproduced from generation to generation and thus has important conservative elements. The mode of its reproduction within the family helps to account for its unconscious dimension, as well as its relationship to the individual's sense of identity. Yet it is not monolithic, for it contains internal contradictions, and those who live within it can disagree about its apportionment of roles and power.

Myths have a dual function within such a system. As traditional stories, handed down from generation to generation, they participate in the reproduction of the gender system and can help people to ignore or to live with its contradictions. Yet myths exist in multiple versions that can reflect the differences of perspective and the struggles for power within the system. It is not necessary, then, for a feminist to take a wholly pessimistic view of mythology, and I will not take such a view here. I believe it is important to uncover the workings of the gender system if we are to improve the lot of women; but this involves celebrating the multiplicity of perspectives within the system as well as criticizing its oppressive aspects. This dual approach – both celebratory and critical – will inform my book as a whole.

Modern interpretations of the *Homeric Hymn to Demeter*

I chose to begin with the myth of Demeter and Persephone not just because it is still popular with modern readers but because it has been studied from many different angles, using the lenses of many different fields of scholarship. Suppose our young friend Sara were to write a research paper about the myth for her university course, focusing on the interpretation of the *Homeric Hymn*. What kinds of published studies would she find? What range of approaches might she encounter?

If she is lucky, or well-advised by her teacher, she may come upon Helene Foley's edition of the *Homeric Hymn to Demeter*.[31] In one volume, she will find an English translation (on facing pages with the Greek text), a line-by-line commentary, and a collection of critical essays, beginning with Foley's own exhaustive interpretation, which includes a review of the major issues raised by earlier scholars. In Foley's commentary and in the footnotes and bibliography to her volume Sara will find references to a whole range of earlier interpretations, including some in Italian, German, and French. On pages 30-1, she will even find a complete list of the major Greek and Latin versions of the myth, some not yet translated into English. Following the leads in the footnotes, Sara identifies a number of earlier works to read; these in turn lead her to others.

The first essay she reads, conveniently included in Foley's collection, is 'Politics and Pomegranates: An Interpretation of the *Homeric Hymn to Demeter*', by Marylin Arthur. Combining literary and psychological approaches, Arthur compares the plot of the *Hymn* with the Freudian account of the 'normal' girl's psycho-sexual development, especially her 'phallic' phase. Arthur makes it clear

38

that she does not accept all aspects of Freud's account, but she draws detailed comparisons between it and the *Hymn* to show that they describe a remarkably similar series of psychological reactions. In Demeter's case these are precipitated by her daughter's rape, whereas in the case of the little girl they are precipitated by the realization that she lacks a penis – and with it, as Arthur notes, the privileges it confers on boys and men. The first reaction in each case is withdrawal: the girl tries to deny her sexuality, while Demeter withdraws from the world of the gods and assumes the appearance of an old woman 'cut off from childbearing and the gifts of garland-loving Aphrodite'.[32] The next reaction in the girl is what Freud called 'penis envy', a desire to possess the male organ; this may be accompanied by hostility to her mother. In Demeter's case, the second reaction is her attempt to adopt a male baby and make him immortal; when the baby's mother interrupts her, she becomes furious with the mother. The final stage in the 'normal' girl's phallic phase arrives when she abandons the desire for a penis and substitutes the desire for a baby. In this phase she is able once again to identify with her own mother. In Demeter's case the third stage is her compromise and reconciliation with the gods, in which she is reunited not only with her daughter but with her mother Rhea. In both sequences the female protagonist at first revolts when faced with the prospect of subordination to a male regime but eventually becomes reconciled to the role she is assigned in that regime. Arthur suggests that the *Hymn* 'could be subtitled "How to be a Mother-Goddess in a Patriarchal Society" ' (216).

Sara's mother, while browsing in a bookstore, finds several recent books about Demeter. Intrigued herself and thinking it may be useful to Sara, she buys one called *Life's Daughter / Death's Bride* by Kathie Carlson.[33] A Jungian therapist who is also a feminist, Carlson believes in the reality of the goddesses – at least in so far as they represent archetypes, elements of 'the objective psyche that is common to us as a species and appears to transcend the boundaries of space, time, and consciousness' (3). In contrast to Arthur's and Foley's detached analytic approach, Carlson describes her personal reactions and those of her clients, urging her readers to 'enter into the myth' and 'experience [its] numinosity and mystery' (7). In at least two ways, Carlson believes, the myth can have healing power for us today as it did for the ancients: it can help us face and overcome the fear of death, and it can help us deal with the psychological effects of patriarchy. She describes two ways of reading the myth (primarily as represented by the *Hymn*). Read with a 'matriarchal accent', it emphasizes the positive nature of the mother-daughter bond and its power to reclaim life from death. Read with a 'patriarchal accent', it emphasizes Persephone's need for a bond with the male as well and for a role in the wider world that can only be achieved by escaping her mother's 'binding' influence. Yet Carlson (like Ann Suter) points out that there is actually little evidence in the *Hymn* for the patriarchal view, beyond the claims of Zeus, Hades, and Helios (the all-seeing sun god) that the goddesses will receive honours in the new regime. Even feminists, Carlson argues, read the myth 'through a contemporary patriarchal filter' that makes maturity contingent on an escape from the mother-daughter bond.

Carlson refers several times to a book edited by Christine Downing, *The Long Journey Home*.[34] Intrigued, Sara looks it up in the university library and finds a collection that contrasts in interesting ways with Foley's. Like Foley's, it begins with a translation of the *Homeric Hymn* and includes a range of interpretive essays, but Jungian psychology is given pride of place and modern poems and short stories are included. Here Sara finds an excerpt from Bruce Lincoln's 1981 book, *Emerging from the Chrysalis: Studies in Rituals of Women's Initiation*.[35] As the title suggests, Lincoln sees the myth of Persephone primarily as the reflection of ancient ritual practice. Unlike most of those who take this approach, however, he argues that the Eleusinian Mysteries – which were open to men – were merely the final form of what began as a puberty ritual for girls. His book analyses a series of analogous rites that were or still are practised by the Navajo, the Tukuna of Brazil, and other peoples. And he cites an impressive number of details in the myth that can be seen as parallel to specific features of puberty rituals: the age of Persephone, who is described as an adolescent; the 'liminal' (transitional) nature of her experience in the underworld, when she has been wrenched from one secure status and has yet to receive a new one; her change of name, from Kore (a generic 'maiden') to Persephone (a personal name); her initiation into sexuality; the 'cosmic' implications of her experience; and her restoration to society in a new adult role. Sara sees a potential contradiction in the argument that Lincoln seems not to have noticed: he insists that Zeus has only benevolent intentions toward Persephone, while at the same time observing that her 'initiation' is accomplished by rape, a 'misogynistic' practice meant to '[teach] her proper submission' to males (78-9).

Extending her research, Sara tries an online database called Diotima: Materials for the Study of Women and Gender in the Ancient World (http://www.stoa.org/diotima), which includes extensive bibliographies as well as course syllabi, translations of ancient texts, and links to other websites. Here she finds a reference to Tina Passman's article, 'Re(de)fining Woman: Language and Power in the *Homeric Hymn to Demeter*'.[36] To use Carlson's terms, Passman sees the *Hymn* as speaking almost entirely with a 'patriarchal accent'. Her analysis is anchored not in psychology but in what she calls 'the sociology of Greek gender relations' (54). Passman sees the *Hymn* as reflecting a shift in prehistoric Europe and the Near East from social systems based on matriliny (which trace descent through the mother) and matrilocality (in which a family lives at the birthplace of the mother) to systems based on patriliny and patrilocality. Citing the work of earlier scholars, including Jane Harrison, Marija Gimbutas, and Gerda Lerner, Passman argues that matrilineal systems tend to be associated with religious systems in which goddesses are predominant; societies of this type tend to foster 'gender complementarity' – with division of labour, but sharing of power – in contrast to the rigid gender hierarchy of the Indo-European peoples, including the Greeks and Romans. The *Hymn to Demeter* portrays the goddess as unaccustomed to, and unwilling to accept, the patriarchal practice whereby the father alone arranges his daughter's marriage. But rather than endorse Demeter's protest, the *Hymn* portrays it as destructive to humanity. Zeus cannot ignore her power over fertility, but he 'tames' it by acting as if it were an 'honour' (Greek *timê*) that *he* is bestowing on her in exchange for her acceptance of his regime. Passman sees the myth as justifying that regime

41

by '[lifting] Demeter and Kore ... out of time, making them *types* for all women' (67). In this view, the myth has an explicit ideological message; it provides what the social anthropologist Bronislaw Malinowski would have called a 'charter' for patriarchy (see Chapter 4).

In her mythology class, Sara learns of an approach called 'structuralism' that originated in anthropology and linguistics but has been applied to classical mythology by a school of French scholars influenced by Claude Lévi-Strauss. Curious to see what a structuralist would make of the *Hymn*, Sara asks her teacher for some references and tackles a difficult but exhilarating article by Froma Zeitlin called 'Cultic Models of the Female: Rites of Dionysus and Demeter'.[37] Although the article focuses on the *rituals* in honour of Demeter, especially a festival called the Thesmophoria, Zeitlin includes the myth in her analysis of what these rituals contribute to the 'symbolic category of femaleness' in Greek culture. She begins by explaining that she has learned from Jean-Pierre Vernant, in whose honour the volume containing her article was published, 'to look at the bewildering variety of rites and myths of polytheistic religion as coherent elements in a logical system of values and practices' (129). Within this 'logical system', which Zeitlin anchors firmly in its historical context, she emphasizes three polarities: concealment versus opening or showing, chastity versus obscenity, and order versus disorder. During the Thesmophoria, the married women of Athens (whose version of the festival is best known) left their homes and camped together, without their husbands, on the hill where the male assembly normally met. They fasted and preserved the strictest chastity but were also required by custom to tell obscene jokes. This paradox corresponds to the fact that Demeter in the myth is 'desexualized' by her disguise as an old woman, yet laughs and is cheered by the sexual joking of Iambe. Her experience parallels that of her daughter, who at first refuses to eat but ultimately, in a symbolic consummation of her marriage to Hades, eats the 'honey-sweet' seeds of the pomegranate. The chaste woman must conceal her body and may also have to repress her desires, but in order to conceive and give birth she must open herself to sexuality. 'The coexistence of [chastity and obscenity] within a single ritual expresses the inherent "double bind" ... [that] demands chastity

42

from the wife and yet insists on her sexual nature' (149). The *Hymn* solves this dilemma by moving it to the divine level and by re-enacting the separation and reunion of Demeter and Persephone. The possibility of their reunion 'denies ... the irreversibility of the linear human pattern and suggests a synchronic perspective in which mother and daughter are not separate entities, but only two facets of a single female figure' (149). Zeitlin's final point concerns the effect of the cult on the women themselves: when they were authorized to enjoy obscenity in the absence of men, did this 'creative transgression' give them power, or did it merely justify men's control of their sexuality by suggesting that they could not control it themselves? Zeitlin does not give a clear-cut answer but suggests that the poles of 'disorder' and 'order' remained in tension.

In an anthropology class, Sara learns of yet another approach to myth interpretation, that of folklore studies. She can find no obvious application of this to the *Hymn* and decides to try it herself in the research paper she is writing. In Foley's volume, she recognizes some elements of the folklore approach in a paper by Mary Louise Lord called 'Withdrawal and Return: An Epic Story Pattern in the *Homeric Hymn to Demeter* and in the Homeric Poems'. Lord is building on the work of her husband Albert B. Lord, a scholar of comparative literature who studied the living oral epic tradition of what was then Yugoslavia and used it to illuminate the Homeric poems. Mary Louise Lord begins by noting that in an oral tradition, 'certain story elements tend to belong together and to recur in essentially the same pattern or grouping of themes' (183). She proceeds to outline a pattern she calls 'withdrawal and return', in which 'the hero (or heroine)' withdraws from action, often in anger, and sometimes in disguise, receives hospitality, is recognized, causes (if only by absence) some form of disaster, returns and is reconciled to those (s)he had left. Lord traces this pattern in detail as it appears in both Homeric epics and in the *Hymn to Demeter*, but she does not deal explicitly with gender differences between Demeter and the male heroes. Sara builds on Lord's plot comparisons to argue that an audience familiar with the pattern would have seen the *Hymn* as emphasizing Demeter's power rather than – or in spite of – the compromise she is forced to accept.

*

Myth interpretation has a long and complicated history, which this book does not attempt to retrace in detail. Scholars in many fields have contributed to it, most notably psychologists, anthropologists, sociologists, historians of religion, and literary critics. 'Classicists' – professors of Greek and Latin – are trained primarily as philologists, that is, as 'lovers of words' whose primary competence is in reading and translating the ancient texts. Some classicists in every age have taken a broader view of their subject, analysing the texts as works of literary art and investigating the social and cultural contexts in which they were produced. In the twentieth century this became the norm for classical research, with the greatest acclaim – and controversy – surrounding scholars who combined a traditional interest in 'what the texts say' with the methods and theoretical perspectives of other disciplines. (For some outstanding examples, see the suggestions for further reading at the end of this book.) Yet some classicists are still resistant to contemporary theoretical approaches, from the study of literature as well as from psychology and the other social sciences.

As academic disciplines become more specialized and as published research multiplies, it becomes harder to claim a competence in fields outside one's own.[38] Specialization has the effect of arousing suspicion that 'outsiders' lack the knowledge to contribute anything of substance to one's own field. As I will show, errors of fact are not uncommon in works of myth interpretation, and such errors are hardly limited to non-classicists. But a few such errors do not automatically invalidate the whole of an argument. In contrast to a work like Geoffrey Kirk's *The Nature of Greek Myths*, which rejects many interpretations because they do not do justice to the uniqueness of Greek myth, I focus on what classicists can learn from other fields precisely because they offer us new angles of vision. This does not mean that I lump all myths together as expressions of universal human truths; I am myself suspicious of universalizing interpretations and offer criticisms of them in the course of this book. But I

44

find that comparative and interdisciplinary work has produced valuable results that justify the emphasis I give it here.

In particular, I would argue that feminist scholarship, which has been interdisciplinary from the beginning, has something to offer every discipline. In most general books on classical mythology and its interpretation, feminist approaches are treated as if they constituted a field of their own, separate from and alternative to the major disciplinary approaches (psychological, anthropological, etc.). Sometimes they are dismissed as 'politically correct' and irrelevant to the ancient cultures. While it is true that feminist scholarship has political implications, there is very little scholarship – even in the 'hard' sciences – that does not. This book is intended as a demonstration that gender is implicated in *every* theoretical approach, and that it was the work of feminist women and men that brought this to our attention. A glance at recent work in fields like psychology and anthropology will demonstrate how profoundly they have themselves been transformed by feminist research. If mythology is inextricably involved in the gender system of a culture, neglect of gender issues is likely to distort the findings of the scholar who ignores them.

2

Psychological Approaches

> Freud, Jung, and their followers have demonstrated irrefuta-
> bly that the logic, the heroes, and the deeds of myth survive
> into modern times. In the absence of an effective general
> mythology, each of us has his private, unrecognized, rudimen-
> tary, yet secretly potent pantheon of dream. The latest
> incarnation of Oedipus, the continued romance of Beauty and
> the Beast, stand this afternoon on the corner of Forty-second
> Street and Fifth Avenue, waiting for the traffic light to change.

Thus wrote Joseph Campbell in the 'Prologue' to his best-known
book, *The Hero with a Thousand Faces* (1949). To the question, 'Why
are we still interested in ancient myths?', Campbell's reply was that
we cannot escape them, for they live within us. All people, in his
view, are born with a repertoire of unconscious *archetypal images*
that reveal themselves in fantasy and dream, and that have been
explored in the myths of all cultures. The people of the modern
industrialized West, who no longer share 'an effective general mythology', must turn to psychologists for help in making sense of their
dreams, their private 'myths'.

Though he never called himself a Jungian, Campbell's view of
myth was most deeply influenced by that of Carl Gustav Jung
(1875-1961). Even today, the two major strands in the psychological
interpretation of myth are those that began with Jung and with
Sigmund Freud (1856-1939). Freud was a mentor to Jung until the
divergence between their theories brought an end to their friendship. While both men saw myths as reflecting the structure of the
unconscious mind, Freud emphasized their connections with pathology, that is, with the maladjusted mind and the sources of its pain,
while Jung emphasized the adaptive and creative functions of

46

myths for 'normal' as well as disturbed people. Both men believed that some structures of the unconscious were universal. But Freud insisted that these had to be recreated in the mind of each individual in early childhood. Jung, by contrast, believed that the 'personal unconscious' recognized by Freud was only part of the picture. It was matched, he thought, by a *collective* unconscious', an inborn set of images or 'archetypes' shared by all people. Late in his career Jung made a distinction between the archetype, an abstract 'predisposition to form images', and the specific 'archetypal images' it generated; but as a sympathetic critic has observed, even in this revised form the archetype is seen as 'a patterning process in the human brain, instinctual and alike everywhere, expressing itself in universal human behaviour patterns, motifs, themes, images, and symbols'.[1]

The disagreement between Freud and Jung over the collective unconscious has implications for the relationship of myth to gender identity. Although both men made universalistic claims for their theories, it has proved much easier to historicize Freud – to see his theory as historically and culturally contingent – without rejecting his basic account of the *processes* by which the unconscious is shaped. Many feminists who reject the 'normality' of what Freud saw as normative femininity and masculinity have not felt compelled for that reason to reject his account of how children acquire these gender identities in modern Western culture. Because Jung, by contrast, believed that some *contents* of the unconscious were universal, his theory has been described as 'essentialist'. Feminists who believe there is such a thing as 'essential' femininity or femaleness – a nexus of qualities shared by all women but not by men – may accept Jung's theory of the archetypes in principle even if they disagree (with him and with each other) about the specifics. Feminists who reject the notion of 'essential' femininity tend to reject Jung altogether. To them, the collective unconscious is a dangerous concept, one that can serve to keep women in their place in an era when they are trying on new roles and forging new identities.[2]

Although I see serious problems with both Freudian and Jungian approaches to the interpretation of mythology, I also think it is impossible to deny that myths affect us at an unconscious level. Why are we drawn to them? What are the sources of the intense *pleasure* they give us, even in heavily 'commodified' and disguised forms such as Disney cartoons? Why do children ask to hear the same stories over and over? Why do certain plot patterns recur, not just in traditional myths but in modern works of fiction and fantasy? Psychological theories can shed light on all these questions.

In an essay on 'The Romantic Appeal of Joseph Campbell', Robert A. Segal makes a distinction between 'rationalist' and 'romantic' approaches to the interpretation of myth.[3] Segal's 'rationalists' see myth as a primitive form of science, an explanation of how the world works that is no longer useful to us because it has been superseded by more accurate scientific accounts. Campbell and his 'fellow romantics', by contrast, see it as eternally valid because it explains not the workings of the physical universe but the nature of 'ultimate reality' as apprehended by the human mind. Although Segal does not put Freud or Jung into either of these camps, his distinction has helped me to see how the two thinkers differ and why their followers have taken such disparate paths. Freud was a 'rationalist' who never took the unconscious as a given but sought to explain how it came to exist under the pressure of external factors such as patterns of family relations and cultural practices. What is more, he never accepted the human need for myth as normal but considered it a regressive tendency caused by our inability to accept life as it really is. Freud rejected not only myth but religion as forms of wish-fulfilment, attempts to return to the state of infantile dependence on parents who could satisfy our every need. Jung, by contrast, saw both myth and religion as positive phenomena. While his theories, like Freud's, had a rationalistic basis, Jung was a 'romantic' in his willingness to accept the unconscious as part of human nature, and human nature as part of a wider reality with which it was not necessarily at odds. It might be added that Jung was an optimist about the human condition, while Freud was pessimistic about both the nature of reality and our ability to accept it.

These tendencies can be seen in many of the later works and schools of interpretation that have built on the thought of Freud and Jung. Freud has had the greater influence on theory in the social sciences and humanities, which have built on his rationalistic 'diagnoses' of the sources of pain and dysfunction in individuals and cultural systems. Jung has inspired a vast literature celebrating the archetypes and offering 'prescriptions' for their use as sources of self-understanding and strength.[4] Although both traditions have contributed to the interpretation of classical myth, the Freudian approach has been more useful to the rationalistically-oriented scholar, while the Jungian – to judge by its popularity – has been more attractive to creative artists and to the general reading public. For this reason, and because Jung borrowed some elements of Freud's psychology, I will describe Freud's approach first and in greater detail.

Freudian diagnoses

When I have taught theoretical approaches to the interpretation of myth, none has met with greater resistance than the Freudian. To be honest, I am myself resistant to many elements of the theory. Why should this be the case? I see two primary reasons. In the first place, Freud practised what has been called a 'hermeneutic of suspicion',[5] that is, an interpretive practice that discounts the overt level of meaning and looks 'beneath' it for what is 'hidden'. He was interested in the *repressed* content of human symbols much more than in their overt content. Since repressed meanings by definition reside in the unconscious, we need the lenses of his theory to see the buried meanings of symbols and myths. To a lover of literature, this practice looks reductive; whatever the pomegranate 'stands for' in the *Homeric Hymn to Demeter*, it stands first of all for the fruit itself, with all its distinctive attributes of size, colour, texture, and taste, and to disregard these is not only to risk misinterpretation but to miss a primary source of pleasure in literary art. To be fair, Freud never claimed that the unconscious meaning was the *only* meaning of a symbol; but in his writing and that of his intellectual heirs, it can seem to be the 'real' meaning.

The second source of my discomfort with Freud, which affects many of my students as well, is his insistence that 'anatomy is destiny', that is, that the 'normal' development of a girl consists of learning to accept her 'lack' of a penis, to overcome her envy of males

49

for possessing that organ, and to desire children as a kind of compensation for it. When I introduce feminist critiques of this position, some students are relieved and jump to the conclusion that they can discount the theory altogether. They are almost equally averse to Freud's account of the Oedipus complex, according to which the 'normal' male child must learn to sublimate his desire for his mother and his hatred of the father who is his rival for her love and attention.

Freudians have an answer for those who so readily dismiss his views: they are simply unwilling to accept the possibility that they themselves have repressed desires of the kind he described, which are branded as shameful by society. Yet if the unconscious is truly *un*conscious – as opposed to what Freud called 'preconscious,' that is, merely latent and capable of being *brought* to consciousness – Freud's own reconstruction of its contents must remain hypothetical. He admitted that his evidence was in the form of 'unintelligible' dreams, and that his most basic premise – that such dreams 'must be ... fully valid psychical [acts], with sense and worth',[6] was in the beginning just an assumption. The credibility of psychoanalysis, he realized, rested on its heuristic value, that is, its ability to make sense of the apparently senseless. Clearly he and his followers believed that his theory was validated by its applicability to the dreams of their patients.

The scientific status of psychoanalysis has always been questioned because the evidence on which it relies is notoriously subjective, derived from dreams and fantasies reported by patients and interpreted by analysts predisposed by their training to look for confirmation of Freudian principles. At one extreme, psychoanalysis has even been compared to a religion – or a mythology – whose claims cannot be proved but are accepted by its devotees as an act of faith. Yet at the same time it has become so widely known to Europeans and Americans (albeit in oversimplified and distorted forms) that it can be considered a part of their common cultural worldview, like the theory of evolution – or the ideology of capitalism, to which Freudian theory has been linked.

Psychoanalytic theory has of course continued to evolve since Freud, partly in response to clinical experience. But it has also

50

moved far beyond the clinical setting to influence philosophical understandings of the mind, with implications for literary theory and cultural studies. In particular, the work of Jacques Lacan and Julia Kristeva, combining a revised Freudian model with a Marxist analysis of subjectivity, has been influential in literary circles. Within the field of classical studies, which has traditionally been resistant to theory of most kinds, psychoanalytic interpretation has always been marginal. Yet those who study mythology ignore it at the risk of cutting themselves off from discussions in the wider academic world and in the popular media, where its validity continues to be debated.

If there are so many problems with Freudian theory, why continue to use it? In particular, why trouble to apply it outside its own domain if its validity is contested even there? From my own perspective there are at least two reasons to take it seriously as an analytic tool. It investigates the origins of gendered identity, the process by which most of us come to see ourselves as centrally, indelibly, 'male' or 'female'. And it asserts a continuity (not a simple equation, but a continuity) between the dreams of the individual and the more widely shared, but no more inherently plausible, fantasies we know as myths: stories that are central to our identities as members of social and cultural groups.

Perhaps the most difficult thing for most feminists to accept is the fact that even widespread awareness of the injustice of women's inequality is not enough to bring an end to that inequality. Of course, many of those who keep women 'in their place' are protecting their own privileges and acting out of conscious political or religious motives; but even among those who sincerely believe that women should have equality of opportunity – including women themselves – there is a resistance to the far-reaching changes in attitudes and practices that would be necessary for full equality. Feminist psychologists who accept Freud's description of early childhood development have argued that this resistance to equality has psychological roots. In the heady days of the 1970s, Dorothy Dinnerstein wrote a passionate book called *The Mermaid and the Minotaur* in which she used Freudian theory against itself to argue that the normative pattern of psychological development Freud had

51

described (and described accurately, in her view) was deeply dys-functional, leading not only to the inequality of women but to the Western pattern of reckless exploitation of the earth's resources.[7] Yet whereas Freud assumed the pattern was immutable, Dinner-stein expressed a qualified optimism that it could be changed if the conditions that produced it were changed. Underlying the pattern is the assumption that infants and young children can be cared for only by women – their mothers or other female caregivers. Dinner-stein argued that in this situation – which has certainly prevailed in most cultures for most of recorded history – children of both sexes develop unconscious patterns of feeling and behaviour that keep women 'in their place':

> For the girl as well as the boy, a woman is the first human center of bodily comfort and pleasure, and the first being to provide the vital delight of social intercourse. The initial experi-ence of dependence on a largely uncontrollable outside source of good is focused on a woman, and so is the earliest experience of vulnerability to disappointment and pain. A woman is the witness in whose awareness the child's existence is first mir-rored and confirmed, the audience who celebrates its earliest acts of achievement. This woman, moreover, is the overwhelm-ing external will in the face of which the child first learns the necessity for submission, the first being to whose wishes the child may be forced by punishment to subordinate its own, the first powerful and loved creature whom the child tries volun-tarily to please. She is, in addition, the person around whom the peculiarly ambiguous human attitude toward the flesh begins to be formed. (28-9)

To grow up, in our current circumstances, is to free ourselves from this position of dependence on a woman (or women, in the case of multiple caregivers). As a result, Dinnerstein argued, most of us harbour even in adulthood an unconscious resentment and mistrust of women in authority, and are predisposed to associate women rather than men with 'fleshly mortality' – including aging and death (36). Thus, for example, we are prepared to accept myths such as those of Eve and Pandora, according to which a woman brought death into the world. If men were to assume an equal role in child care, the psychodynamics of family life would be forever altered and women would no longer be available as scapegoats for *human* fallibility and mortality.

Whether or not we accept all the details of Dinnerstein's analysis (which are clearly anchored in Freudian theory), it offers – in contrast to most Jungian approaches – a diagnosis of dysfunction in the gender system that is based on potentially changeable social arrangements rather than immutable inborn archetypes. Freudian readings of myths are also more apt to acknowledge the dysfunction and pain that result from gender conflicts, whereas Jungian readings tend to see conflict as a means to greater ultimate integration or 'wholeness' of the personality. If women are currently finding more *therapeutic* value in Jungian approaches, I would argue that theories descended from Freud's offer better *diagnoses* of dysfunction in our gender system, which if heeded might lead to real social change.[8]

Since Freud focused most of his attention on the dilemma of the male child, rather than that of the female child or the parent of either sex, it is not surprising that his theory works best when applied to myths of male heroes or the 'younger' generations of male gods. Hero myths, and the rare classical myths that – like the tale of Cupid and Psyche – feature the coming of age of a female protagonist, share a family resemblance with folk and fairy tales, which have also been interpreted from a psychoanalytic perspective.[9] Jungians are equally concerned with myths that reflect the maturation process. Thus the interpretations I will consider in this chapter focus on stories in which the protagonists, whether divine or human, are portrayed as children or young adults.

Before turning to these detailed interpretations, it may be useful to summarize a few of the central principles of Freudian theory, since despite its widespread influence it is often misrepresented and misunderstood. Two components of the theory are especially relevant to the interpretation of myths: Freud's account of human psychosexual development and his method of interpreting dreams.

According to Freud, the unconscious is inaccessible to us (except in dreams) because it is *repressed*. The process of repression – itself unconscious – is a normal and necessary part of socialization, a defence mechanism by which we deal with 'prohibited, dangerous, and anxiety-provoking thought and behaviour of childhood'.[10] Contrary to popular belief, Freud did not think children were interested only or primarily in sex; rather, he thought that a large part of the unconscious, formed in infancy and childhood, consists of sexual desires and fantasies because these are the most restricted by social norms and the most threatening to the dependent child's developing personality. Moreover, the term 'sexuality' is used by Freudians in a broader sense than ordinary usage would suggest, to refer to 'all activities, wishes, and fantasies that aim at producing a specific organic pleasure and that cannot be adequately explained in terms of a basic physiological need such as breathing, hunger, or excretion'.[11] The so-called 'erogenous zones' of the body are those that provide such pleasure, and the child becomes aware of them in a typical order: for the infant, the focus is the mouth ('oral' phase); for the toddler in toilet training, the anus ('anal' phase); and for the child of three to five, the genital area ('phallic' phase). (A branch of psychoanalysis known as 'object-relations theory', which became prominent in the 1950s and 1960s, points to the ways in which culturally-specific child-rearing practices may shape what Freud took as a 'natural' sequence.)[12]

The 'oedipal' phase, to which Freud attached such importance, coincides with the 'phallic' phase and is, in psychoanalytic theory, the decisive stage in the formation of the child's sexual identity. The two names attached to this phase show clearly that it was conceptualized from the point of view of the male child (though the complementary term 'Electra complex' – also borrowed from Greek mythology – was coined for the girl's experience). This is the stage at which children become curious about parental sexuality and their own genital anatomy. Freud thought that because males have penises and females do not, children of both sexes fantasize that the mother and the little girl are 'castrated'; the boy fears that he may suffer a similar fate, while the girl experiences 'penis envy'. The solution for the boy is to repress his desire for the mother which threatens to throw him into a conflict with the father that he could not win; the girl must learn to replace her desire for a penis with the desire for a child. Very early in the history of psychoanalysis – beginning in Freud's own lifetime, with the work of Karen Horney – women analysts asked whether there might not be such a thing as 'womb envy', and pointed out that what the girl desired was not so much the boy's anatomical organ as the social privileges to which it gave access. Thanks to the work of many feminist psychologists and theorists,[13] these corrections seem to have been accepted by most analysts. Further modifications to Freud's theory of identity formation have come from the 'object relations' school, which puts more emphasis on the infant's relationship to the mother in the first year of life.

The interpretation of dreams has always been a focus of psychoanalysis because dreams are one of the few windows on the unconscious. Yet although repressed thoughts and emotions can find expression in dreams, they tend to be heavily disguised. Freud identified a number of processes by which the 'latent content' of a dream (its unconscious substratum) is transformed into its 'manifest content' (the dream as 'seen' by the dreamer). These processes are essential to the psychoanalytic interpretation of myths and other literary forms that share the fantastic quality – and perhaps some of the functions – of dreams. *Condensation* is the process by which several, or even many, different mental images are represented by a single image in the dream. A common example in the modern world is to dream of taking an exam for which one has not studied: the exam serves as a distillation of many different sources of anxiety. A mythic equivalent might be a combat in which the hero faces overwhelming odds of defeat. *Displacement* is the process by which an emotion attached to one object in the latent content is shifted to an apparently unrelated object or image in the manifest content. Displacement takes many forms; *symbolism* – the representation of one object (or person, or idea) by another – is an obvious one; others include *decomposition* or splitting, by which one object is divided into two or more (such as the 'good' and 'bad' mothers of the typical fairy tale); *projection*, by which a strong or threatening emotion felt by the dreamer is attributed to another figure in the dream; and *reversal*, in which an idea or emotion is replaced by its opposite. An example of projection in myth is the desire of Phaedra or the biblical Potiphar's wife for a younger man, which can be read as a reflection of the *hero's* (= the son's) repressed desire for a mother-figure. An example of reversal is the revulsion attached to the snaky-haired Medusa's head: in one interpretation, it stands for the mother's genitals, which the child wishes (but also fears) to see.

Because of the essentially *disguised* nature of the dream content according to Freudian theory, the challenge is to arrive at the proper interpretation for a given patient. This requires skill on the part of the analyst and cooperation on the part of the dreamer, who must provide the personal associations with which specific images are freighted. Freud warned repeatedly that there could be no recipe book for the interpretation of dreams, since the same image can have very different associations for different dreamers. This difficulty is obviously magnified in the case of myths, which must have meaning for a large population. The mechanism of reversal further complicates things, as a quote from Freud makes clear: 'An element in the manifest dream which is capable of having a contrary may equally well be expressing either itself or its contrary or both together.'[14] Thus hatred of a father figure might stand for hatred, or for love, or for ambivalence. Perhaps it is not surprising that psychoanalysis has played an important role in literary theory, and been rejected as 'unscientific' on the same grounds as literary criticism. Both enterprises focus on inherently ambiguous products of the human mind; and both have an irreducible subjective component – a stumbling block to anyone whose model is the 'hard' sciences.

Perhaps the most detailed psychoanalytic reading of a Greek myth is Richard Caldwell's *The Origin of the Gods*, which focuses on Hesiod's *Theogony* but includes supporting examples from the whole corpus of Greek mythology. Acknowledging the opposition in classical circles to the approach he has chosen, Caldwell wryly observes, 'I hope that those who have not yet made up their minds will agree, at least, that psychoanalysis should have something to say about a myth in which the first father [Ouranos] marries his mother and is then castrated by his son' (10). The *Theogony* cannot be seen as its author's personal fantasy, since it is based on earlier oral traditions, some traceable to the Near East; it was then widely adopted by later Greeks as an authoritative account of the origin of their gods. Caldwell attributes its success to the 'striking psychological logic' (164) with which it portrays the rise of Zeus, the youngest male god of his generation, to the position of supreme ruler and 'father of gods and men'. Each of the first two male gods to claim supremacy – Ouranos and Kronos – is overthrown by his son (Kronos, Zeus) with the aid of his wife (Gaia, Rhea). Ouranos, like Kronos and his siblings the Titans, is portrayed as gigantic in size – another clue that the myth is based on an infantile fantasy (145). Zeus is able to end the pattern of succession by preventing *his* first wife, Metis, from giving birth to the one son who might have overthrown him.[15] His 'oedipal triumph' complete, he is free to marry his sister Hera and to couple with a long series of goddesses, nymphs, and mortal women, producing numerous sons who are no threat to his rule. Logically, Hesiod's poem had to account for a religious system in which Zeus was the supreme and permanent ruler. But in Caldwell's view, 'underlying the logical inevitability of Zeus' triumph is an emotional imperative that is no less compelling. Zeus is victorious ... because he is, at least in the *Theogony*, not so much the archetypal father as the idealized son' (186-7). Of course, Zeus does not marry his own mother; to that extent, at least, he must be seen as sublimating his oedipal desires, though in one Orphic fragment (58) he does couple even with Rhea.

Caldwell obviously assumes, though he never states this outright, that a Greek hearing or reading Hesiod's poem would be most likely to identify with its protagonist, Zeus, *in his role of son.* This assumption is congruent with Freud's that the focal figure in the Oedipus story is the son. As a literary critic, I have to agree that the point of view most fully represented in the *Theogony* is that of Zeus, and in Sophocles' *Oedipus Rex* and *Oedipus at Colonus*, that of Oedipus. Provisionally, then, let us assume that psychoanalytic theory can contribute something of importance to the interpretation of these works and of other surviving works from the ancient world whose protagonist is portrayed as a son. This approach has in fact been the basis of most psychoanalytic studies of classical myths. I will focus on two of the most influential, that of Otto Rank (*The Myth of the Birth of the Hero*, 1909), as modified by Caldwell, and that of Philip Slater (*The Glory of Hera: Greek Mythology and the Greek Family*, 1968[16]), each of which focuses on the male hero in relation to his parents.[17]

A striking feature of the 'hero pattern' is the hostility the infant hero often faces from a father-figure; thus Oedipus is exposed to the elements at his father's orders, Perseus at the orders of his grandfather, and Romulus and Remus at those of their great-uncle. Rank interpreted this as a projection of the *son's* hostility to the father who is his rival for the mother's affections: by fantasizing that the father seeks to destroy *him*, the son absolves himself of guilt at the unconscious wish to get his father out of the way. Of course Oedipus and Romulus are, from a modern perspective, imaginary figures, who *ipso facto* can have no unconscious desires to project; this interpretation rests on the (often unstated) assumption that the *audience*, and perhaps the teller, of the typical hero-tale has such desires. Caldwell nuances his interpretation by pointing out that there are often *two* father-figures, one good and one bad; this can be explained by the phenomenon of decomposition or splitting, which helps the son deal with his ambivalent feelings toward the father (he does not feel hate *only*, but love as well).[18] Thus Jason has a good father (Aeson) but a bad uncle (Pelias); Romulus and Remus have a good grandfather (Numitor) but a bad great-uncle (Amulius); Perseus has a bad grandfather (Acrisius), a good adoptive father (Dictys), and a persecutory father-figure who pays court to Perseus' mother (Polydectes). Of course, for many heroes – including Romulus and Remus and Perseus – the ultimate 'good' father is a god, whose only involvement is to beget the hero and look down in distant pride at his son's achievements. Such a hero must usually be raised by foster-parents of inferior rank – a fantasy replicated in the modern hero-tale of Superman and in modern children's adoption fantasies.[19] This form of splitting helps the child (still conceptualized as male) reconcile his initial inflated estimate of his parents' powers with a later, more realistic view of them.[20]

Another 'oedipal' feature of the hero pattern is the virginal status of the mother and the mysterious circumstances of the hero's conception. Danae, Perseus' mother, is imprisoned in a tower (or an underground chamber) and impregnated by Zeus in the form of a 'shower of gold'; the mother of Romulus and Remus, Rhea Silvia, is a Vestal Virgin mysteriously impregnated by the god Mars. As Alan Dundes points out in his article tracing the hero pattern in the life of Jesus, 'a son who is born of a virgin can deny that his father ever had sexual access to his mother'.[21] Perseus enjoys a special monopoly on his mother, cast adrift with her in a floating chest (which Dundes reads as a fantasy of protracted nursing) and performing his later feats to defend her against the unwelcome advances of King Polydectes. Yet the mother too has 'good' and 'bad' sides, and the gentle Danae is balanced by the fearsome Medusa, whom Perseus must kill. Jocasta has her monstrous counterpart in the Sphinx, who like her commits suicide when Oedipus has solved the riddle of his identity.[22]

Philip Slater's analysis of the Greek heroes and male gods focuses almost entirely on their relationships with their mothers, which Slater believes reflect a pathological pattern in ancient Greek culture. He begins with the often-observed paradox that the ancient Athenians, who kept 'respectable' women in seclusion and drastically limited their legal rights, produced some of the most powerful portrayals of women in world literature. Because women in classical Athens (from which he draws nearly all his evidence for cultural practices) were excluded from the public sphere and its privileges but in charge of the home, Slater reasons that while they may have had little to do with their husbands, they must have loomed large in the experience of their young sons. Though frustrated themselves and envious of their sons' (future) masculine privileges, they would also, in Slater's view, have seen a son as an available love-object – in contrast to the emotionally distant husband – whose eventual success in the wider world could be a source of vicarious satisfaction. The mother's *ambivalence* in such a situation – the combination of exaggerated love with envy and hostility inspired by the son's masculine privilege – would have produced a reciprocal ambivalence in the immature son: a heightened oedipal attraction combined with intense fear of the mother's adult sexuality and a hostility to match her own.

Slater's analysis of the Perseus myth can serve as a good example of his approach. He begins with a summary of the myth, culled from a variety of sources (of widely varying dates). Building on Freud's identification of the Gorgon's head as a symbol of the female genitals, Slater argues that the myth's 'themes of feminine awesomeness, of frozen staring, of confinement, of impotence, of flight, suggest a peculiarly Greek primal-scene fantasy – one which focuses almost exclusively on the *mother's* sexuality' (309). Danae's impregnation by Zeus in the abstract form of golden rain, and her imprisonment with her infant son, first in a sealed chamber and then in a floating chest, have the effect of keeping father figures out of the picture and exaggerating the closeness of mother and son. Perseus' exploits are motivated by the desire to keep his mother for himself when an older male authority figure (Polydectes) takes an interest in her. What he accomplishes by beheading Medusa, in Slater's view, is to separate the mother from her frightening aspect – her sexuality.

Slater compares Perseus to Superman and other modern super-heroes: 'an apparently weak or helpless individual has or obtains superhuman powers with which he defeats his many enemies and amazes the crowd' (324). (This description would also fit many of the folktale heroes analysed by Dundes and Bettelheim; see n. 9.) Especially striking is the juxtaposition of details that suggest the hero's power with others that qualify that power. The fact that the hero can fly is an expression of phallic potency,[23] and he defeats a variety of human and superhuman foes; yet he needs the help of many divine beings and magical objects to approach his first victim safely. This contradiction suggests the insecurity of the hero, or rather of the implied (male) audience member who will identify with him. His use of his shield as a mirror in which Medusa can safely be watched further suggests the child's mixture of desire to look at the mother's body and fear of looking (and being seen).

Slater also tackles the difficult question of whether the beheading of Medusa symbolizes an act of intercourse, or of murder, or both. Sexual elements include the phallic flying, the fact that Medusa is sleeping when Perseus approaches her, and the fact that after being decapitated she gives birth through her neck to Chrysaor and Pegasus; but parallels to the figure of Orestes, especially the fact that Perseus is pursued by the surviving Gorgons just as Orestes is pursued by the Furies, suggest an act of matricide. Slater notes that in the Jungian interpretation of Erich Neumann, the beheading is a truly heroic act by which Perseus faces and overcomes his maternal dependence, freeing his libido (symbolized by the winged horse Pegasus) and enabling him to seek a bride. While acknowledging that this is a useful interpretation of the hero pattern as a whole, Slater remains sceptical that it can make sense of the myth of Perseus, since Perseus never really 'faces' Medusa and never allows his mother Danae to marry, even after his own marriage to Andromeda.

Slater is a sociologist by training, and his work has been ignored by many classicists: it received only one review in a classical journal in the first ten years after it was published. When it has been noticed, responses have tended to be harshly critical. I can see three reasons for this. The first is a methodological problem: Slater selects details from very different versions of each myth, of drastically different dates and genres, as long as they support his argument (for Perseus, e.g., he cites Hesiod, Pindar, Apollodorus, and Pausanias, who span a nine-hundred-year period); yet the 'Greek family structure' as he postulates it is based on historical evidence for fifth- and fourth-century Athens only. This is a serious problem, but it does not necessarily negate all of Slater's points unless – and this is the second point – psychoanalytic theory is inapplicable to ancient Greek culture as a whole. The feminist classicist Page duBois has taken this view, arguing that Freudian psychology is so anchored in the bourgeois family and the capitalist mode of production that it becomes a distorting lens if applied to the ancient world, preventing us from seeing what is truly 'other' about ancient gender systems.[24] Unfortunately, while duBois analyses a number of Greek *symbols* of female sexuality, she does not offer a reading of the *plots* of Greek myths that might refute a Freudian reading such as Slater's. The Marxist classicist Peter Rose, on the other hand, has combined a Freudian reading of the *Odyssey* with a detailed analysis of its social and historical context, showing that these approaches are not necessarily incompatible.[25]

The third, and to my mind the decisive, reason for hostility to

Slater is that he explores frankly, and sometimes seems even to relish, the 'nasty' aspects of Greek myth: incest, rape, and violence of every kind, including murder. This makes for some uncomfortable reading, perhaps especially for a classicist trained to revere the ancient texts and the culture that produced them. Slater exacerbates the problem by using a frankly pathological clinical parallel (that of a child-molester) for the emotional bind of the *typical* Greek male, and by sometimes adopting a sensational tone; thus he speaks of Hera's 'reptilian hatchetwoman, Python'[26] in the *Homeric Hymn to Apollo*, of the 'vicious oral sadism' conveyed by Clytemnestra's nightmare of Orestes as a snake in Aeschylus'*Libation Bearers*, and, in the *Eumenides*, of Apollo's 'phallic boastfulness and sexual contempt barely concealing the most profound dread of women'. A contemporary reader is also likely to take offence at Slater's reliance on a discredited view of male homosexuality as pathological and as induced by 'bad mothering'. Yet when all this is said, Slater still deserves credit for a pathbreaking study of the gender dynamics of Greek hero myths. Many of the details of his analysis ring true even when the tone is offensive. And surely the offensiveness is not all Slater's – he did not invent the overt gender conflict, violence, and misogyny that characterize so many of the myths. Indeed, his evidence, coming as it does from every era of ancient Greek culture, suggests that the 'pathology' he describes was not confined to fifth-century Athens. And as we have noted from the beginning, the myths did not die with the culture that produced them but were transplanted into Latin literature and have persisted in various forms up to the present day. We could postulate that their meaning has been so thoroughly altered in this process that no continuity of psychological content can be assumed. Yet despite radical changes in family structure, the family in these later cultures has remained patriarchal and child care is still relegated to women. Growing up still means separating oneself from a mother whom one both loves and resents and (in the case of a boy) successfully negotiating a conflict with the father who has been one's successful rival. Parallels to the classical hero pattern in European folklore and in contemporary popular fictions such as the Harry Potter books and comic books suggest that a similar psychological configuration may underlie all these genres.[27] This is not to claim that nothing has changed, just that some important things have stayed the same.

Feminists have a further bone to pick with Slater – and not just Slater but Caldwell and others who have applied the psychoanalytic model to Greek myth. This is the tacit assumption that the myths, and the literature in which they are embodied, can be read *only* from a masculine point of view, whether it be that of a male character, narrator, or audience member. As I have noted, in many psychoanalytic readings the viewpoint is narrower still, being confined to that of the son in relation to his parents. While it cannot be denied that most versions do emphasize the masculine perspective, since they were composed by men for a primary audience of men, this exclusive focus neglects important features of the texts themselves. For a modern audience, it has the further effect of reifying and reinforcing the masculine perspective as the only one, or the 'correct' or 'scholarly' one.

In Caldwell's account of the castration of Ouranos, for example, much is made of the fact that Ouranos, having married his mother, must be wary of his sons doing the same; but all Hesiod says is that Ouranos 'hated' his children (line 155) and 'took pleasure' in the 'harmful deed' of hiding them inside Gaia. It is *Gaia's* pain, ignored by Caldwell, that precipitates the castration: groaning and full to bursting, she creates a new material, fashions it into a sickle, plans the ambush, and appeals to her children to carry it out, emphasizing that it was their father who began the conflict (lines 159-66). Only Kronos is bold enough to take up the challenge, and he too insists his hostility is a response to Ouranos' prior outrage (170-2). This *could* be read as an ingenious double projection from the son's point of view – attributing pain to the mother that further justifies retaliation for the hostility he has projected onto the father. But virtually all the agency in the story is Gaia's, except for the actual deed of castration (which, if the attack is to be an ambush, cannot be performed by her). This fits Slater's scenario of the frustrated wife looking to the son for satisfaction. But if it is not read entirely from the son's point of view, as *his* fantasy, it can be seen as an acknowledgment that the wife has real grounds for resentment – that she has been outrageously treated by her mate and is justified

63

in taking revenge. She is also portrayed as resourceful even in distress, and as vastly more intelligent than the son/husband who is crudely oppressing her. Her cleverness may be used for trickery, but if Kronos is 'crooked of counsel' (as his chief epithet asserts), it must be from Gaia and not from his oafish father that he inherits it.

Kronos in turn becomes his wife's oppressor, this time explicitly to prevent his own overthrow. And although he finds a somewhat better scheme than his father's – swallowing his children as each is born – he too fails to reckon with his wife's 'unforgettable grief' (467) and is outwitted by her, with the help of Gaia (and, surprisingly, Ouranos). While Gaia takes the baby Zeus to be reared in a cave on Crete, Rhea gives Kronos a stone wrapped in baby clothes, which he promptly swallows. Zeus quickly grows to manhood and, again with the advice of Gaia, compels Kronos to regurgitate the stone and the other children. Granted that Zeus is the winner in all of this, and that his point of view predominates in what is left of the poem, Hesiod can also be seen as giving expression to Gaia's and Rhea's perspectives as aggrieved wives and mothers. Women in his audience, both ancient and modern, do not find an entirely one-sided version of the battle of the sexes. This myth can also be interpreted as a thinly-disguised expression of 'womb envy' – male envy of the female capacity to give birth. In each generation the supreme male god does a better job than his predecessor of mimicking female reproduction, until Zeus succeeds in appropriating the entire process by swallowing Metis and giving birth to Athena himself.[28]

The first half of the *Homeric Hymn to Apollo*, the so-called Delian Hymn,[29] likewise focuses on the female perspective of Leto, Apollo's mother, and portrays both solidarity and rivalry among goddesses. Slater, concerned with the figure of Apollo, notices contradictory images suggesting the son's ambivalence about maternal attachment: he is surrounded by nurses (all the goddesses except Hera are present at his birth) and '[shows] some reluctance to leave his mother's womb' (she is in labour for nine days and nights); yet once born, he is not nursed by his mother and bursts his swaddling bands, acquiring his adult attributes immediately (Slater, 138-40). This is a perceptive reading, yet it ignores the fact that the *Hymn* opens with Leto's own perspective – a description of her joy and pride in her son and the solicitous care with which she greets him, takes his bow and quiver, and offers him nectar each time he returns to the hall of the gods (lines 1-13). In fact, Leto's attitude is contrasted with that of the other gods, who all fear Apollo and jump up from their seats at his approach; only Leto remains seated. In the birth narrative that follows, she also reassures Delos (who is personified as female, since all islands are feminine in Greek) that Apollo will not scorn or abandon her if she agrees to be his birthplace. The implication is that Leto can speak for her son; she even swears a great oath that Delos will be the most honoured of Apollo's sanctuaries. There is a tension in the birth narrative between female solidarity, expressed by the presence of many goddesses, and female rivalry, since Hera – jealous of Leto – not only stays away herself but detains Eileithyia, the goddess of childbirth. The other goddesses must bribe Eileithyia to come and release Leto from her labour. (While Slater suggests that Apollo is reluctant to be born, the *Hymn* focuses instead on *Hera's* reluctance to *let* him be born.) Hera's jealousy of Zeus' many consorts is usually thought of as sexual jealousy, but in the *Hymn* she is explicitly said to be envious of the fact that Leto is about to bear a 'distinguished and strong son' (99-101). Since Hera's own sons, Hephaistos and Ares, are considerably lower than Apollo in the Olympian hierarchy, it may be as a mother rather than as a wife that Hera resents Leto, at least in the *Hymn*.

The Delian section of the *Hymn to Apollo* is unusual in giving an explicit description of its audience, which is said to include the women as well as the men of Ionia, and in particular a group of unmarried girls, called the handmaidens of Apollo (156-64), who perform in the god's honour. Their songs praise Apollo first, then Leto and Artemis, but they also 'remember' the men and women of the past, and they themselves are said to deserve undying fame for their skill. It is suggestive that one of the few ancient poems to acknowledge the presence of women as audience members and performers also gives so much weight to the perspective of its female characters. To be sure, Leto is praised as the mother of a *son*, while Apollo's twin sister Artemis is barely mentioned; but there is a glimpse of the 'female world' of the birth chamber, where women gather to assist and celebrate a uniquely female achievement. At the moment of birth they raise the *ololugmos*, a ritual cry of triumph (119).

The mother's perspective, then, is not entirely missing from our texts; it is central to the *Homeric Hymn to Demeter*, considered in Chapter 1, and many examples could be cited from later periods, such as the figure of Creusa in Euripides' *Ion* or the Sabine women in Livy. As a feminist classicist and literary critic, I can identify gaps like these in psychoanalytic readings of mythic texts. But it is powerful testimony to the value of interdisciplinary research that some of my central insights have come from anthropologists and literary theorists outside the field of classics.

In an article entitled 'The Indian Oedipus', A.K. Ramanujan describes an initially frustrating search for Indian parallels to the Oedipus myth that ended in one such revelation.[30] After looking in vain for masculine figures who could be compared to Oedipus, Ramanujan was conducting fieldwork in a North Karnatak village when an old woman, herself illiterate, told him a folktale that fully paralleled the Oedipus story – except that the protagonist was the Jocasta figure! It was *she* who received the prophecy that she was to marry her own son, she who tried in vain to escape her fate and who at last discovered that it had overtaken her. Ramanujan went on to find several other variants of this tale type in oral and written forms. None of them involve parricide, and several actually have a happy ending: the mother does not reveal the situation to her son/husband and continues to live happily with him! Moreover, Ramanujan found that 'this story is told invariably by women and to girls' (241). One version was collected by a woman anthropologist, Irawati Karve, whose little daughter accompanied her; it was to the daughter that an older woman addressed the tale. His eyes opened by this discovery, Ramanujan looked again at the corpus of Indian mythology and found many more stories whose plots could be compared with the Oedipus myth – except that the protagonist was the father, the Laius figure, and violence was usually inflicted by father on son rather than the other way around. In some cases, the son chooses to renounce his own sexuality and youth so that his father's life and youth may be prolonged. These plot types seem to reflect deeply rooted patterns of deference to elders in Indian culture.

2. Psychological Approaches

An analysis like Ramanujan's can help the classicist to see how and why certain aspects of female (and male) experience are elided in surviving mythic texts from the classical world. The shift of focus from a Western to an Eastern culture, combined with the shift from masculine to feminine perspective, is a salutary reminder that psychoanalysis, created by a man and his mostly male successors in western Europe and North America, incorporates cultural as well as gender biases. Some of these parallel the biases of Greek and Roman myth as it has come down to us – without many traces of a 'women's tradition' that might give us a very different view.

In *The Mother-Daughter Plot: Narrative, Psychoanalysis, Feminism*,[31] Marianne Hirsch, a literary critic, arrives independently at a closely related conclusion about the difficulty we face in trying to look at fiction or theory with a mother's or a daughter's eye. These perspectives have been elided from mainstream fiction and scholarship for so long that even feminists may not notice their absence, or may be uncomfortable with what they find when they begin to look. Hirsch adds the important observation that psychoanalysis itself provides a narrative which many of us have internalized and which teaches us how to 'read' our own experience: 'The family romance [a Freudian term for the child's adoption fantasies] is the story we tell ourselves about the social and psychological reality of the family in which we find ourselves and about the patterns of desire that motivate the interaction among its members' (9). In this way, psychoanalysis does function as a kind of modern myth – a story, shared by successive generations within the same culture, that describes the way things are and explains how they got to be that way. It may not be accidental that Freud based the linchpin of his theory of psychosexual development on a Greek myth; he has certainly done more than any other individual to keep that myth alive in the modern world.

Jungian prescriptions

Unless we unthinkingly accept the modern usage by which 'myth' equals falsehood, the recognition that psychoanalysis has a mythic dimension need not prevent us from finding truth in it. Yet this recognition brings us back to the question (mentioned at the beginning of this chapter) of the relationship between myth and the status quo. Some Freudian interpreters of myth – notably Caldwell and Bettelheim – do not limit themselves to the diagnostic approach but assign to myth a therapeutic function.[32] Caldwell points out that laboratorary research has found dreams essential to mental health; building on the Freudian analogy between myth and dream, he concludes that 'just as individuals seem to need their own idiosyncratic dreams and private rituals in order to prevent anxiety and preserve sanity, it would seem that societies need shared myths and public rituals to maintain the emotional integrity and collective health of the group' (17).

It is the Jungians, however, who have gone farthest in developing the therapeutic potential of myth. For them, as for Freudians, the 'hero pattern' is a model of individual psychosexual development. But where the Freudians saw pathology, Jungians tend to see a natural growth process governed by inborn 'archetypes' we all share. Thus myths can be of positive help to the individual who, consciously or unconsciously, is following the path they blaze. Joseph Campbell goes even farther, suggesting with Nietzschean fervour that the heroic quest is one to which we can still aspire. This is because the journey is an inner one, a descent into the unconscious, from which the hero returns with insights that can reinvigorate an entire culture. In Campbell's more colourful prose, 'The effect of the [hero's] successful adventure ... is the unlocking and release again of the flow of life into the body of the world' (40).

In Jungian theory, the psyche or personality matures by becoming aware of the archetypes, entering into dialogue with them, and integrating them into the 'self'. In its special Jungian sense, the self is the most important archetype, 'the supreme psychic authority', a kind of 'inner ... deity' with the power to orchestrate both conscious and unconscious elements of the personality.[33] The self is distinct from the ego, the centre of *conscious* identity, which is overdeveloped in a rationalistic culture and even encouraged to deny the reality of the unconscious. In a society where there is only one religious tradition, 'each individual projects his inner God-image (the Self) to the religion of the community'.[34] In modern secular societies, by contrast, the individual is more likely to become alienated from the self and must be reintroduced and reconciled to its unconscious components.

Some of these essential components are also archetypes: the shadow, the *anima*, and the *animus*. The shadow is the nexus of impulses which we repress because we are taught to see them as negative or frankly evil, but which we must bring to consciousness lest they act in us without our knowledge. The *anima* is the man's unconscious image of the female; the *animus* is the woman's unconscious image of the male. These last two archetypes are the most deeply problematic from a feminist perspective, since Jung's view of them was shaped by the sexism of his own cultural milieu. In particular, he associated the intellect with the male and the emotions with the female, implying that until a woman had come to terms with her *animus* she must be ill at ease in the intellectual sphere, while a man needed his *anima* to put him in touch with his emotions.

Joseph Campbell tries hard to show that the composite 'hero pattern' can accommodate female as well as male heroes; the fact that he taught at a women's college may have helped to motivate this egalitarian claim. At almost every stage of the hero's career, Campbell includes examples of female figures from world mythology who can be seen as passing through that stage. But the situations of these female figures are not always truly comparable with those of the male heroes. A striking example from classical myth is that of Daphne (as described in Ovid's *Metamorphoses*), whom Campbell describes as 'refusing the call to adventure' by running away from the god Apollo. When she sees that she cannot escape, Daphne appeals for help to her father, a river-god, who transforms her into a tree. Campbell sees in this 'dull and unrewarding finish' a father-fixation preventing the girl from breaking out of 'the walls of childhood' (62). But the long passage from the *Metamorphoses* – which he quotes in full – makes it clear that Apollo is not inviting Daphne to embark on an adventure but pursuing her as a hound pursues a hare (the simile is Ovid's). Surely rape is not one of the dangers commonly faced by male heroes in the myths,[35] nor would it be likely to start Daphne on a heroic career; rather, the typical pattern for the heroine raped by a god is to bear him *sons* who become heroes, while she herself fades from the scene.[36]

Campbell has much less trouble finding female figures who play the role of helper or guide – or conversely, that of 'threshold demon' (a 'dangerous presence dwelling just beyond the protected zone' of the hero's home ground). In Greek and Roman hero myths a female character is seldom the protagonist – the central figure around whom a story revolves and whose perspective on the action is most fully represented.[37] One of the few human female figures who can be said to undertake an adventure comparable to those of the male heroes is Psyche, the heroine of a 'story within the story' in the Latin work of Apuleius called *The Golden Ass*.[38] Campbell cites her as an example of the hero undergoing initiatory 'trials', but even he admits that in her story, 'all the principal roles are reversed: instead of the lover trying to win his bride, it is the bride trying to win her lover; and instead of a cruel father withholding his daughter from the lover, it is the jealous mother, Venus, hiding her son, Cupid, from his bride' (97-8). In fact, the tale has many elements in common with fairy tales in which a girl is the protagonist, such as 'Cinderella' (the wicked, task-setting stepmother and sisters), 'Sleeping Beauty' (the sleep of death), and the less-known 'East of the Sun and West of the Moon' (the perilous journey). (For a summary of the plot and a comparison with 'Beauty and the Beast', see Chapter 6.) These parallels have led scholars to assume that the Psyche story had folktale antecedents, although the highly literary version of Apuleius is the only one to survive from the classical world. Perhaps because it is atypical for a classical myth, the story has attracted many interpreters, including a disproportionate number of Jungians.

In its Apuleian version, the tale is on some level an allegory: because Psyche means 'soul' (or 'mind' or 'spirit') in Greek, her adventures are a metaphor for the vicissitudes of every soul, like those of Christian in Bunyan's *Pilgrim's Progress*. But because she is also a female character, like the heroines of the related fairy tales, her story has been seen by Jungians as an allegory of the 'psychic development of the feminine' (the subtitle of Erich Neumann's commentary). The sheer number of different meanings that Jungians have seen in the tale casts doubt on the usefulness of the archetypes as guides to the *content* of myth. But this same range of meaning reveals the degree to which Jungian interpretation is a subjective and creative *process*. As we have seen with Freud, any interpretation of a myth risks participating in the ideological functions of myth itself, but Jungian interpretations have sometimes self-consciously spilled over into active myth-making. This may explain why, despite their 'essentialist' aspects, they have been more appealing to feminist therapists and their patients. I will consider two Jungian readings of the Psyche myth, one of which reveals the worst anti-feminist tendencies of this school and one of which involves some feminist re-writing of the myth.[39]

Erich Neumann's *Amor and Psyche: The Psychic Development of the Feminine*, appropriately published in the 1950s, is a masterpiece of 'pedestalian' thinking – a paean of praise to the 'truly feminine' woman whose maturation consists of defining her relationship to the 'masculine' as embodied in her future husband.[40] ('Through Eros, through her love of him, Psyche develops not only toward him, but toward herself', 110.) The book is written in a deeply obscure style well-suited to the mystification it perpetrates, and in fairness to the author, he seems to have been as mystified as anyone:

> It is true that innumerable women consummate marriage or perform the act of childbearing without going through the corresponding 'experience' – as, to our surprise, we often observe in modern women – but this does not do away with the marriage situation as an archetype and central figure of feminine psychic reality. Myth is always the unconscious representation of such crucial life situations, and one of the reasons why myths are so significant for us is that we can read the true experiences of mankind in these confessions unobscured by consciousness. (65)

In other words, the myth tells us what we should be feeling; if we don't feel it, the problem is with us, not with the myth.

In striking contrast to Campbell's view of the hero's journey as one that takes him *into* the depths of the unconscious, Neumann

71

portrays Psyche as '[emerging] from the darkness of her unconscious' by breaking Eros' command and gazing on him in the light. This ends her 'sexual servitude' to him; but it also hurts him and causes a prolonged separation, during which she learns – through a series of symbolic tasks set by Venus – to approach the 'overpowering energy' of 'the masculine' indirectly and at the appropriate time (the evening, when the masculine sun has set!), so as not to be destroyed by it. The various helpers who come to Psyche's aid represent aspects of her unconscious; in particular, the eagle, the bird of Zeus, is associated with the *animus*, the 'masculine' component of the woman's unconscious in Jungian theory. Neumann makes it clear that although Psyche's trials require her to develop this masculine side, she is fundamentally unlike the male hero in two ways: her quest is undertaken solely for love; and paradoxically, her ultimate victory is based on failure. When she opens the casket that she thinks contains a beauty lotion (to restore her desirability) and is overcome by a deathlike sleep, Eros comes to her aid: 'Through the perfection of her femininity and love she calls forth the perfect manhood of Eros' (125).

Reading this at the start of the twenty-first century, we are struck by Neumann's sexism.[41] But two details of his interpretation have feminist possibilities that have been developed by subsequent writers. He points out that the interference of Psyche's sisters, though motivated by ill-will, has a good effect, forcing Psyche out of dependence on Eros and setting her on the road to further development. (The harsh tasks set by Venus, a mother-figure, have a similar effect.) Further, to complete her final task – a journey to the underworld – Psyche must resist the temptation posed by pathetic figures who appeal to her for help; as Neumann puts it, 'the feminine is threatened in its ego-stability by the danger of distraction through "relatedness" ' (115).

Jean Shinoda Bolen, a Jungian therapist and author of highly popular self-help books such as *Goddesses in Everywoman* (1984), had no classical background when she was introduced to the Psyche myth by Neumann's book in the late 1960s.[42] She found that her female patients 'took heart from a myth that mirrored their situation ... and gave a larger meaning to their struggle'. Recognizing that this myth 'spoke to women who put relationships first', she went on to investigate the very different figures of Atalanta (who competed successfully with men) and of the Greek goddesses, in whose diversity Bolen found a metaphor for the range of women's psychic strengths and vulnerabilities. Bolen is a true Jungian in that she believes in the existence of the archetypes; as she puts it, 'Archetypes exist outside of time, unconcerned with the realities of a woman's life or her needs' (*Goddesses*, 285). But she is also a feminist, who helped organize Psychiatrists for the Equal Rights Amendment and persuaded her friend Gloria Steinem, who had some initial misgivings, to write a foreword to her book. Bolen believes there is a difference between archetypes and stereotypes, 'the roles to which society expects women to conform' (4). In contrast to Jung, who identified women's capacities for independent thought and action with the masculine *animus*, Bolen equates them with the independent virgin goddesses Artemis and Athena, insisting that there is nothing inherently 'masculine' about them (259). *Awareness* of the archetypes, or of the inner 'goddesses', gives women some control over them; myth interpretation can be a form of therapy, combining intellectual and intuitive insight.

Not surprisingly, Bolen picks up on Neumann's idea that 'related-ness' can be a stumbling block for women when they try to set independent goals. Spelling out the implications of Psyche's predica-ment, she says women must 'learn to say no' to those who would derail their projects with demands for attention or assistance. With-out voicing any overt criticism of Neumann, she jettisons the worst of his sexist assumptions and reads Psyche's other tasks as straight-forward self-help strategies: sorting a mixture of seeds is a metaphor for sorting out 'a jumble of conflicted feelings and compet-ing loyalties' before making an important decision; getting the fleece of dangerous rams means getting power without getting hurt or losing one's own sense of priorities in the process; and the soaring flight of the eagle who helps Psyche obtain water from a stream guarded by dragons represents the ability to 'get some emotional distance' on a relationship.

It seems clear that for Bolen, her patients, and her large audience of readers, classical mythology is at once a source of validation and a body of material that is 'good to think with'. As Bolen puts it, 'When a woman senses that there is a mythic dimension to something she is undertaking, that knowledge touches and inspires deep creative centers in her' (6). While Bolen may be the best-known spokesperson for this view, she is scarcely alone in it; in fact, her book has spawned a whole new self-help genre, including her own *Gods in Everyman* (1989). Classicists have largely ignored this literature, which is full of misrepresentations of classical sources, but – as in the case of Joseph Campbell – we are probably the beneficiaries of its popularity. Some of the students flocking to our myth courses probably first met the goddesses in books like these, which have the merit of treating the myths as something we might still be able to 'think with'.

There is however an implicit contradiction in a feminist Jungian reading that equates the Greek goddesses with archetypes. For as Bolen herself admits, these goddesses 'lived [*sic*], as we do, in a patriarchal society' (23). If they are inborn in every woman, then we are in some sense 'programmed' for patriarchy; but Bolen insists this is not the case. The contradiction becomes evident when, in *Gods in Everyman* (300-3), Bolen must struggle with the question whether a new archetype can come into existence as men assume new nurturing roles in the family. She imagines this archetype as 'the missing god', son of Zeus and Metis, 'who was to supplant his father … and rule with an all-loving heart' (295). (The classical sources never make the latter claim.)

It is not surprising that when she looked for powerful female figures in Greek myth, Bolen quickly settled on the goddesses as opposed to the mortal women. In place of Neumann's view that there is a single normative pattern of female 'psychic development', Bolen emphasizes the multiplicity of the goddesses, which she uses as a metaphor for the complexity of the individual female psyche as well as for diversity and conflict among 'real' women. The male gods too are multiple, providing a greater range of psychic models than the 'monomyth' touted by Campbell.

2. Psychological Approaches

Missing persons

What – or rather, who – is still missing from this picture? We have already noted the silence of most classical myths about the mother's perspective and about the ties between mother and daughter; still deeper is the silence about lesbian desire. Even the mythic women who were said to have expelled men from their midst – the Amazons – or to have killed them wholesale – the Lemnians – were not portrayed as forming love relationships with one another. This bespeaks an overwhelming taboo in a culture that produced many myths about incest of all sorts and about parents killing, even eating, children. There are quite a few myths involving male same-sex desire,[43] and the supreme gods Zeus and Apollo, like the hero Herakles, are allowed male love-objects; but the one surviving classical myth involving erotic love of one woman for another – that of Iphis for Ianthe in Ovid's *Metamorphoses* (9.666-797) – portrays it as unnatural and features a 'happy ending' in which Iphis is turned into a man. This erasure, which persisted in Western culture until very recently, was noted in feminist critiques of Freudian theory beginning in the 1970s; some ground-breaking studies were those of Hélène Cixous and Luce Irigaray in France, and that of Adrienne Rich in the United States.[44] It should not surprise us that lesbian poets and thinkers, who found their experience elided from both the Western literary tradition (with its roots in classical mythology) and the leading Western models of psychological development, were the most radical critics of traditional stories and of the mainstream psychological readings of them. Cixous mounts an especially vivid attack on both:

By dint of reading this story-that-ends-well, [woman] learns the paths that take her to the 'loss' that is her fate. Turn around and he's gone! A kiss, and he goes. His desire, fragile and kept alive by lack, is maintained by absence: man pursues. As if he couldn't have what he has. Where is she, where is woman in all the spaces he surveys, in all the scenes he stages within the literary enclosure? ... Kept at a distance so that he can enjoy the ambiguous advantages of the distance ...

75

But doesn't [men's] fear [of women] suit them fine? Wouldn't the worst thing be – isn't the worst thing that, really, woman is not castrated, that all one has to do is not listen to the sirens (because the sirens were men) for history to change its sense, its direction? All you have to do to see the Medusa is look her in the face: and she isn't deadly. She is beautiful and she is laughing.[45]

From this perspective many myths, far from contributing to 'mental health', help to maintain a gender system that is dysfunctional as well as sexist. For Cixous and many other contemporary women – of varying sexual orientations – the solution is to re-write the myths. The recent burgeoning of poetry, fiction, and scholarship from lesbian perspectives suggests that the former erasure of these perspectives is not evidence of their absence in former times but of social and cultural norms that branded them as deviant.[46] The silence of mythology in this case seems to show that myth cannot be *only* a reflection of the unconscious structure of the human mind; it must also have deep normative functions rooted in social structure. In my next chapter I turn to myth-and-ritual theories that focus on these functions. I will not lose sight of the psychological interpretations but will continue to invoke them as alternatives or supplements to other theoretical approaches.

3

Myth and Ritual

The psychological approaches are not the only ones to focus on myths about a young person's coming of age. Since the early twentieth century a number of scholars, beginning with a group called the 'Cambridge School', have seen such myths as reflections not of individual psychological development but of 'initiation rituals', religious rites designed to mark the transition of an individual or group of young people from childhood to adult status. Initiation is the most prominent, but not the only, form of ritual used to account for the narrative patterns and the otherwise puzzling details of myths. In recent decades the ancient practice of animal sacrifice has become a focus of intense interest and debate, partly because of its assumed connection to the 'hunting hypothesis' of human evolution. Myths that tell of human sacrifice, and especially maiden sacrifice, have been interpreted in the context of this larger discussion. In the work of Walter Burkert and René Girard, sacrifice is identified – and justified – as a distinctively human, and exclusively masculine, form of killing that served to keep male violence within bounds. Burkert links sacrifice with initiation, claiming that the shared act of killing served to induct young men into the adult community.

Critics, including feminist critics, of such theories have pointed out that they too have a mythic function: by positing an innate male tendency to violence, they normalize that tendency and justify the institutions of patriarchy and warfare as necessary controls on it. In rebuttal, feminist anthropologists have developed their own theories of the interaction of biological and cultural evolution. At the same time, a growing number of classicists, including many women, have also taken a closer look at *women's* rituals in ancient Greece and Rome. Because ritual practices, like other social functions, were often segregated by gender in these cultures, women's religious experiences must have been significantly different from men's. In particular, women's initiation rites – which seem to be reflected in many classical myths – would have differed because the roles of adult women were so different from those of men. As in so many other facets of life, the evidence for women's ritual practices is fragmentary and scattered. The myths are better preserved than any other form of evidence, so that interpreters tend to rely heavily on them. Independent evidence for the details of ritual, however, is often lacking, as are any firsthand accounts of what women's rituals meant to the participants. Most classicists therefore resist the temptation to reconstruct the women's perspective, but the popularity of fictions that do so, from Christa Wolf's *Kassandra* to *Xena: Warrior Princess*, testifies to the desire of modern women for mythic prototypes of their own experience. Smaller groups of feminists have self-consciously developed mythologies, and even rituals, of their own as alternatives to patriarchal traditions. A surprising number of these take classical myths as their point of departure, as did some of the Jungian therapies discussed in Chapter 2.

The so-called 'myth and ritual' approaches differ greatly among themselves, but they share an emphasis on the *social* dimension of religious practices. Human beings live in groups – extended families, clans, city-states – which perpetuate themselves by reinforcing their common ties in periodic ceremonies. Such ceremonies affirm, in symbolic form, the solidarity of the group and the values or ideologies its members are supposed to share. Myths, too, affirm values, and this common function suggests the possibility of a common origin, especially when mythic plots seem to echo details of known ritual practice.

Most classicists who use this approach have borrowed heavily from the field of cultural anthropology. In particular, they seek to apply the techniques of ethnography, or detailed description and interpretation of cultures, to the evidence from classical antiquity. Inevitable problems arise when a method developed for the study of living cultures is applied to the fragmentary evidence of ancient ones. But while 'ritualist' interpretations of many specific myths have been challenged, the questions raised by the method have greatly invigorated classical scholarship. Early practitioners of the myth-and-ritual approach met with intense opposition from more conservative colleagues, partly because the new approach seemed to be demoting the classical cultures from their privileged status as models by equating them with 'primitive' cultures in the modern world. And these opponents were not altogether wrong: the use of anthropological models has in fact taken Greek and Roman cultures down from the pedestals they once occupied, treating them as equivalent rather than superior to the array of other human cultures, past and present. At the same time anthropology has revealed the 'otherness' of classical cultures, that is, the profound differences between them and modern Western cultures, which older, more adulatory approaches tended to ignore. By *defamiliarizing* Greek and Roman culture this approach has done much to reshape – and to revitalize – the entire study of Classics.

From the perspective of this book, the myth-and-ritual school is notable for its explicit attention to gender differences; girls and boys are destined for different roles in most cultures, ancient and modern, and the rituals – or lack of rituals – to mark their coming of age reflect these differences. Men and women also had markedly different roles in the ancient practice of animal sacrifice. A young, unmarried girl, the *kanephoros*, carried the basket in which the knife was hidden, but the knife was almost always wielded by a man, and men were in charge of the division of meat.[1] Even at the all-female Thesmophoria festival a man was brought in to do the actual slaughtering of the animal victims. In mythology, which often describes human sacrifice, the sacrificers again are male,[2] but the victims, usually portrayed as willing, are more likely to be female.

Initiation and sacrifice are the two forms of ritual whose connection with mythology – and with each other – I explore in this chapter. I look first at the pioneering work of the Cambridge school and then at some more recent work on the same issues. The structuralists, who also treat these issues in anthropological perspective, have such a distinctive approach that they deserve a chapter of their own.

Jane Harrison and the Cambridge School

As it happens, one member of the Cambridge school, arguably its most important member, was also the first woman classicist to acquire an international reputation. Jane Ellen Harrison was one of the first generation of women to be admitted to a British university: she was one of only twenty residential students in Newnham College, Cambridge, when its hall opened in 1875.[3] Although she had been tutored at home and attended a girls' school, she did not have the rigorous background in classical languages that her male peers had received as a matter of course. As Robert Ackerman puts it, 'she suffered throughout her life from having begun the study of Greek relatively late, and despite her obvious *Sprachgefühl* [feel for languages], she never was as competent a philological scholar as she would have wished to be'.[4] Not until the age of 48 did she obtain an official academic post, again at Newnham. Despite the fame she earned for her books, she was a controversial figure in her own lifetime, drawing the attacks of some established classicists.[5] There followed a long period in which her work was largely discredited and forgotten. While this was also true to some extent of her fellow 'ritualists' J.G. Frazer, Francis Cornford, and Gilbert Murray, their reputations have fared better. Even since the rediscovery of her work in the 1970s, appreciations of it have been personalized in ways that suggest her gender is still an important factor in her reception. At a symposium on the ritualists held in 1989, William M. Calder III devoted an entire paper to proving that Harrison was *appropriately* twice passed over for a professorship.[6] Robert Ackerman, one of the most generous of her champions, foregrounds her personal relationships in a way that he does not do for her male colleagues:

> Harrison was, at every period of her adult life, always connected in a deeply emotional way with some male scholar of superior philological attainments who acted as a technical adviser and, just as importantly, as an essential emotional support.[7]

3. Myth and Ritual

At the same time, however, Ackerman explicitly acknowledges the issue of Harrison's gender and goes so far as to suggest that her socialization as a woman contributed to her achievement, since 'then as now, ... men were not permitted the same range of emotional expression as women' (70). Not only did she serve as a facilitator, bringing together by her friendship scholars who might otherwise never have met, but she was prepared to admit the role of emotion in religion – one of the ritualists' major insights. With no prospect of a career in philology, she educated herself in archaeology and art history while reading voraciously in the newly emerging social sciences. With this breadth of knowledge, which made her suspect to some critics as a non-specialist, she became one of the first classicists to do truly interdisciplinary work. Reading her at the turn of the twenty-first century, a classicist cannot help but be struck by the fertility of her mind and by the large number of current hypotheses and controversies that are anticipated in her books. A non-classicist may be somewhat intimidated by her mass of detailed evidence, yet the sprightly and impassioned style makes her works more accessible than many scholarly tomes.

While Harrison is seldom credited with the invention of the myth-and-ritual theory, H.S. Versnel has shown that she published a version of it simultaneously with the two male scholars who are given pride of place in most accounts: W. Robertson Smith (*Lectures on the Religion of the Semites*) and J.G. Frazer (*The Golden Bough*).[8] In its earliest formulation (1890), her view was that 'in many, even the large majority of cases *ritual practice misunderstood* explains the elaboration of myth'.[9] Like many nineteenth-century scholars, Harrison was seeking to trace the origin and evolution of the phenomena she studied. Anthropology was in its infancy, and thinkers like E.B. Tylor and Henry Morgan had recently posited a series of universal 'stages' of religious belief or technological progress through which most cultures were thought to pass in sequence. Thus Harrison reconstructed a hypothetical evolution in Greek religion from a stage of 'totemistic thinking', in which humans identified vividly with the rest of animate nature, to a belief in *daimones* or spirits who were in essence projections of the group of worshippers, to a belief in more individualized heroes and finally in the fully individualized Olympian gods. Interestingly, Harrison was ambivalent about whether this evolution represented real progress. She paid much more attention to the earlier stages, and sometimes described the Olympians as 'chilly' idealized figures, even 'objets d'art'. She also accepted the view of J.J. Bachofen that matriarchy, or at least matriliny (the reckoning of descent through the mother), had preceded patriarchy in the evolution of social systems. This historical sequence, she thought, was reflected in the evolution of prehistoric Greek religious beliefs, which had found expression in Greek myths. As Tina Passman has noted, Harrison's belief in prehistoric matriarchy must have inspired some of the enduring prejudice against her work. The fact that she had passionate friend-ships with women as well as men may also have aroused prejudice.[10]

The first of Harrison's two major books, *Prolegomena to the Study of Greek Religion* (1903), was devoted to ritual, as she sought to recover the more ancient and 'primitive' cults that had preceded but still influenced the classical worship of the Olympian gods. Her next book, *Themis* (1913), had more to say about myths. By this time she had read the French sociologist Emile Durkheim and shifted the emphasis of her research to 'the social origins of Greek religion' (the subtitle of *Themis*). Now she argued that myth had arisen simulta-neously with ritual, as 'the spoken correlative of the acted rite'. At first, a myth (which can mean 'word' in Greek) might consist merely of the words spoken during the ritual; 'as man is a speaking as well as a motor animal, any complete human ceremony usually contains both elements, speech and action'. But like ritual action, which is 'not simply a thing done but a thing *re*-done or *pre*-done . . . under strong emotional excitement and done collectively', myth is 'a re-utterance or pre-utterance, it is a focus of emotion, and uttered ... collectively or at least with collective sanction'. This special kind of speech could easily evolve, Harrison thought, from a kind of running commentary on ritual action to a parallel narrative or 'plot' (*Themis*, 328-31).

The mythic plots on which Harrison focused were variations on a basic pattern outlined by Frazer in *The Golden Bough*: the selection, by contest, of a 'Year-King'; his eventual defeat; and his resurrection or replacement. The 'king' might be an actual leader or a ritual substitute. Both sacrifice and initiation are connected to this pattern, since the death (actual or symbolic) of the 'Year-King' can be seen as sacrificial, while his younger successor is a kind of initiate. In fact, for Harrison, the 'king' and his successor represent one and the same person. She believed that in ritual practice, the death was purely symbolic: the initiate 'died' to his old status and way of life and was 'reborn' into a new status – usually that of adult. Only in the myth that developed out of the rite was the death a literal one. Harrison saw this pattern behind a great many Greek myths, including those of the heroes Hippolytos, Herakles, and Theseus, and even of the gods Apollo, Dionysos, and Zeus himself. Since the Greek gods were immortal by definition, such a move was self-consciously paradoxical on Harrison's part. In her view, the fully anthropomorphic Olympians were latecomers to Greek religion, preceded by, and still resembling, the hero-*daimones* (hero-spirits), who originated as projections of the group of young male worshippers. As Harrison put it, 'The worshippers ... are prior to the god. The ritual act ... is prior to the divinity' (*Themis*, 29).

The key example she offered was that of the Kouretes, a band of young men who in myth preserved the baby Zeus from his father's hostility, concealing his cries with the clash of their war-dance. In a Cretan hymn that may date to the Hellenistic period, Zeus is hailed as 'greatest Kouros' ('greatest of the young men') and asked to 'come to Dikte for the year' and 'leap' with his worshippers for the increase of flocks and fruits. Though the hymn itself is late, Harrison saw it as the best evidence for her thesis that the god is in origin a projection of the worshippers themselves. She saw a Roman parallel in the aristocratic priesthood of the Salii, or 'leapers', associated with the god Mars, whose spheres included the fertility of crops as well as victory in warfare.

Harrison admitted that the pattern of contest, death, and resurrection that she traced in so many myths was in itself monotonous, like the similar (and, she thought, related) pattern of the mummers' play still performed in her time by country people throughout Europe to mark the new year or the change of seasons. In Greece, the myths, in the sense of words spoken in connection with a rite, very early 'cut themselves loose' from the ritual context (*Themis*,

334). This allowed them to develop the complexity and variety we associate with the plots of Homeric epic and Athenian drama.[11] In Harrison's view, it was only after myths had become detached from their original ritual contexts that they came to be thought of as 'aetiological', that is, as explaining the origin or cause (*aition*) of a ritual. Thus the story of Zeus' birth, which grew out of the ritual dance of the Kouretes, came to be cited as the reason or precedent for it.

Like most ritualists of her time and ours, Harrison seldom gave a sustained interpretation of an entire myth; instead she used details of many myths to illustrate her theses about the history of religion. Because her account of Dionysos is especially detailed, I will use it as an example, both of her method and of her views on initiation and sacrifice.[12] Dionysos, like the Zeus of the Kouretes' hymn, is himself a *kouros*, a young man, and even a baby in myth. The dithyramb, a circular dance for boys or men, is his equivalent of the dance of the Kouretes or Salii.[13] Yet he is also associated with groups of *women*, the Bacchants or Maenads. What is their relationship to the god? Harrison argues that in origin they are his nurses. 'The Bacchants are the Mothers'; this is why, as vividly described in Euripides' *Bacchae*, they can make springs of milk, honey and wine flow from the earth (*Themis*, 40). They worship not only Dionysos but Rhea, a divine mother-figure. This emphasis on the mother-son tie suggests to Harrison that the worship of Dionysos originated in a matrilineal era, when descent was traced through the mother. King Pentheus, who in myth opposes the Maenads as women out of control, represents the patriarchal values of a later age.

Yet if Dionysos has a surplus of mothers, the myth also describes him as born of a male: when his human mother Semele is killed before his birth, his father Zeus undertakes to carry the fetus to term in his own thigh. Harrison sees this second birth as a reflection of tribal initiation rites designed to separate the boy from the mother:

The birth from the male womb is to rid the child from the infection of his mother – to turn him from a woman-thing into a man-thing. Woman to primitive man is a thing at once weak

84

and magical, to be oppressed, yet feared. She is charged with powers of child-bearing denied to man, powers only half understood, forces of attraction, but also of danger and repulsion, forces that all over the world seem to fill him with dim terror. (36)

In this view, Harrison anticipates several of the more recent interpreters of male initiation. Acknowledging that the attitude she describes is not limited to 'primitive' man, she adds: 'The attitude of man to woman, and, though perhaps in a less degree, of woman to man, is still to-day essentially magical.'

Dionysos is also associated, at least in myth, with the ritual practices of *sparagmos* and *omophagia* – 'tearing apart' a sacrificial victim and 'eating the flesh raw'. The Maenads in the *Bacchae* dismember a herd of cattle; later in the play, they also dismember Pentheus, though they do not eat him. Harrison saw such myths as reflecting the 'totemistic' phase of culture, in which a group of humans see themselves as intimately related to a species of animal or plant. While in most circumstances they refrain from eating this 'totem', at special times they break the taboo and consume it in a communal setting to obtain the power they attribute to it. Indeed, there was a myth in which Dionysos himself was dismembered and eaten by the Titans, only to be resurrected. He was also said to assume animal forms, or animal attributes such as the horns of a bull; his Maenads wore the fawn-skin – a way of identifying with the animals they had killed.

Although the concept of totemism as a phase of human culture has since been discarded, the idea that humans identify with sacrificial animals has not. Along with several other ideas of Harrison's, it has resurfaced in the work of later ritualists.

The 'hunting hypothesis' and its critics

A scholar who clearly acknowledges his debt to Harrison is Walter Burkert, an eminent Swiss classicist born in 1931.[14] One of his most influential books is titled *Homo Necans: The Anthropology of Ancient Greek Sacrificial Ritual and Myth*.[15] *Homo necans* is Latin for 'man the killer'; this is the characteristic of *homo sapiens* ('man the knower') that Burkert singles out for study. ('Man' in Burkert is not generic but really does mean 'male', as he occasionally acknowledges.) Like the French-born American literary critic René Girard, whose *Violence and the Sacred* was published the same year as *Homo Necans* (1972), Burkert argues that sacrifice played a central role in the history of culture, not just the classical or ancient Mediterranean cultures but all human cultures since the Palaeolithic era. Both men are biological determinists who see the roots of sacrifice in the innate aggression of human males; both cite the work of animal behaviourist Konrad Lorenz, *On Aggression* (1963), in support of their claims. Not only do their theories have clear implications for the past and future of gender relations, but both men explicitly discuss those implications. These two scholars and their feminist critics have provided one of the most interesting chapters in the history of twentieth-century thought – not to say twentieth-century mythology.

Burkert and Girard, though writing half a century after the Cambridge school and coming from very different traditions, are nonetheless clearly 'ritualists' because they insist on the priority of ritual and trace its imprint in myths, drawing most of their examples from ancient Greece. Burkert cites examples of ritual behaviour among non-human primates as evidence that ritual must have preceded myth because it can exist without language. Yet it resembles language in seeking to communicate, and even to 'dramatize', feelings; thus the two work together. Whatever the origin of myth, once it appeared, myth and ritual 'were transmitted together because they explained and strengthened each other' (*Homo Necans*, 33).

The radical claim of both Burkert and Girard is that sacrificial ritual was the crucial step in the creation of human society. Girard sees the sacrificial victim (animal or human) as a scapegoat who allows the members of a group to vent their aggressive impulses without turning against one another. Burkert finds the origin of social bonding in a more complex sacrificial pattern of aggression followed by reparation, which he traces back to the rituals of Palaeolithic hunters. Just as those early hunters – and their descendants in modern hunter-gatherer cultures – sought to placate the prey by reassembling its bones, sacrificers in Greece and Rome collected skulls at the place of sacrifice. The elaborate rituals that grew up around hunting and then were transferred to animal sacrifice were meant both to expiate the hunters' guilt at the taking of life and to ensure the *continuity* of life – the replenishing of the food supply. Burkert claims that sacrifice became a part of funerary ritual precisely because of its symbolic juxtaposition of death and survival: 'In the experience of killing one perceives the sacredness of life; it is nourished and perpetuated by death. This paradox is embodied, acted out, and generalized in the ritual' (38).

Both Burkert and Girard also make connections between initiation and sacrifice. Because sacrifice dramatizes and reaffirms social hierarchy, those on the verge of adulthood must assume their proper places by taking part in a sacrificial ritual. In rites of passage, the young may at first be cast as 'substitute victims', subject to bullying or hazing. Ultimately, however, young *males* must be enlisted as 'successors' (Burkert's term) who will perpetuate the system. Warfare, which also serves to integrate young men into the system, is itself a form of ritual, 'symbolically interchangeable' with hunting and sacrifice: 'a self-portrayal and self-affirmation of male society' (*Homo Necans*, 47).

Burkert's reading of the myths about Dionysos is startlingly like Harrison's. Like her, he sees the myth of the Titans' dismemberment and eating of the baby Dionysos as reflecting a prehistoric initiatory ritual involving sacrifice (probably animal sacrifice). The scarcity of evidence for such a ritual in historic times leads Burkert, like Harrison, to rely on parallels with other gods. As she used the Hymn of the Kouretes, addressed to Zeus, to reconstruct the worship of Dionysos, he uses parallels between Dionysos and Apollo, who were brothers in myth and who shared the shrine of Delphi. Neither scholar is bothered by the indirectness of the evidence because both assume that ritual is something older than the belief in individual, named gods; in this perspective the figures of Zeus, Apollo, and Dionysos are to some extent interchangeable.

In a chapter eerily titled 'Werewolves around the Tripod Kettle', Burkert reconstructs a ritual of Apollo celebrated in historic times on Mount Lykaion in Arcadia, at which a stew of sacrificial flesh was shared by a fellowship of young men, a *Männerbund*. Plato reported the story that a piece of a human victim was included in the stew and whoever ate that piece was transformed into a wolf; Pausanias (second century CE) adds that if the wolf refrained from eating human flesh for nine years, he regained his human form. Citing the parallel of 'leopard men' in African tribal societies, Burkert reads the Greek story as a mythic version, or gloss, of an initiatory ritual for boys requiring them to spend time in the wild or the 'bush'. The animal transformation, combined with the period of exile on the margins of society, suggests that the myth and ritual complex is ultimately related to hunting: 'By training himself in the ways of the wolf, man became a hunter and lord of the earth' (89). Burkert traces similar patterns in rituals and related myths from other sites in Greece, concluding with Delphi where, according to Plutarch (first-second century CE), an elite male priesthood performed an 'unspeakable' sacrifice associated with the dismemberment of Dionysos. At the same time, 'Thyiads' – women acting the part of Maenads – performed a ritual described as 'waking Liknites' (an infant – presumably Dionysos – who has a winnowing-fan as a cradle). As in Harrison's interpretation, the Maenads are cast as nurses, and initiatory sacrifice sets the community of men apart from that of women: 'The *Männerbund* is juxtaposed to the company of "raving" women; the act of killing in the shrine corresponds [*sic*] to caring for the newborn child in the female realm' (125).

But Burkert looks farther back in time than either Harrison or Girard to link his theory to the 'hunting hypothesis' of human evolution – the view that male hunting in groups was the decisive behavioural adaptation leading to the evolution of distinctively human traits such as erect posture, tool use, and language.[16] According to this model, the gendered division of labour goes back very far indeed, so far that it can be seen as encoded in our genetic makeup. In order to hunt, the story goes, hominid males needed a larger brain to compensate for their lack of claws, tusks, and muscles that could make them a match for the larger mammals. The larger brain in turn required human infants to be born at an earlier stage of development, so that they needed a longer period of care before being able to fend for themselves. In this view, while early hominid males travelled widely in search of big game, the females stayed close to home, caring for infants and children and supplementing the group's diet by gathering more accessible forms of food. In some versions of the theory, the nuclear family, with man as 'breadwinner' – actually meatwinner – evolved at the same time. Since hominid females, unlike other female carnivores, did not hunt themselves, they were dependent on permanent bonds with males who would be willing to share their 'take'.

Burkert (like Girard) assumes a biological link between aggression and male sexuality. Since hunting required temporary abstinence from sexual relations with the homebound females, human killing became 'sexualized'. Myths of maidens sacrificed before battles, such as those of Iphigeneia and the daughers of Erechtheus, reflect 'the strongest form of the attempt to renounce sexuality' (64). The Greek divinities who preside over hunting and warfare, Artemis and Athena, are portrayed as female because stimulation of aggressive impulses also arouses sexual desire; but these goddesses are virginal because the sexual urges must be deferred until after the hunt or battle.

The 'hunting hypothesis' grew up and flourished in the 1950s and 60s. Ironically, just as Burkert and Girard were publishing their work in the 1970s, the hypothesis was being challenged and revised by anthropologists. Bone deposits that had been taken as evidence for early hominid hunting were reinterpreted as evidence of scavenging, while hominid bones that had been thought to prove early cannibalism were now seen as the discards of carnivorous animals.[17] According to the new consensus, early hominids did not hunt; there was still disagreement about the time when a sexual division of labour emerged, but big-game hunting had developed too late to shape our genetic inheritance. Meanwhile, with the entry of more women into the field of anthropology, the neglected females of the species were being taken more seriously. Had they really played no part in human evolution? Soon the figure of Man the Hunter was joined, and even displaced, by that of Woman the Gatherer.[18] If female hominids had in fact been made less mobile by their childcare duties, this would not have kept them from foraging. Language and food-sharing were at least as likely to have developed from the interaction of mother and child as from the interaction of hunting males. In their gathering or foraging role, women may well have been the inventors of such essential but perishable 'tools' as baskets for food storage, string for nets and traps, and baby carriers to keep their hands free while they worked. Clearly, human intelligence is not a sex-linked trait, and the assumption that hunting required more intelligence than foraging or child care was the product of a deep androcentric bias. Even the assumption that men do all the hunting was shown to be false: in most hunter-gatherer societies, women hunt small animals, and in a few they hunt larger game as well.[19] By a curious coincidence, 'Woman the Hunter' is not unknown to Greek mythology: the goddess Artemis was herself an enthusiastic hunter, like her protégée Atalanta; and the Maenads, when they were not nursing Dionysus, were known to hunt and dismember wild animals. Yet classicists have refused to see in these myths any reflection of actual human practices. Why are we willing to project werewolves and 'leopard men' into prehistory but not women hunters?

Feminist anthropologists have done more than initiate a study of women's roles in the past. They have also pointed out some ways in which modern Western gender roles and hierarchies shape scholars' *visions* of the past. Surely it is no coincidence that when Western researchers of the 1950s and 60s imagined human beginnings they pictured adventurous male 'meatwinners' in pair bonds with sedentary, dependent females. The prominence of weapons and violence in the 1950s account of how we became human made sense to a generation that had just fought a world war and was involved in armed conflicts in Korea and Indochina. Implicitly, such an account justified an escalating arms race. In the Cold War era it was also ideologically convenient to claim as a common universal ancestor an entrepreneurial hunter whose economic and family structures could be seen as proto-capitalist.[20]

By the same token, it is not surprising that feminists themselves picture a distant past in which women's contributions are more prominent. This pattern of a suspiciously close fit between scholars' images of the past and their ideological commitments in the present is unlikely to be the result of conscious distortion. Nor should it be seen as simply negating the value of their work. Rather, it is testimony to the quasi-mythic power of a story about origins to legitimate our institutions in the present and our visions of what the future may hold. Anthropologists may now see 'Man the Hunter' and 'Woman the Gatherer' as oversimplifications, yet as Mary Zeiss Stange has argued, these mythic figures are 'alive and well' in the popular media and in contemporary movements such as ecofeminism and the 'men's movement'.[21] Hard as scholars may try to eliminate mythic patterns from their theories, these tend to reassert themselves in subconscious ways, especially in popularizing versions. In the secular culture of the post-modern West, many people look to scholars, especially scientists, for validation of their world-view, including their views of gender relations. In an age when these relations are being thoroughly renegotiated, it is small wonder that scientific theory should assume for us some of the functions of aetiological myth. (I discuss this further in Chapter 4.) Scholars vary in their willingness to admit the presence of mythic patterns or functions in their research: cultural anthropologists tend to be relaxed about it, while historians and sociobiologists often deny it outright. Classicists, who employ many methodologies, may be found at both ends of this spectrum and at various points in between. Those of us who focus on literature and are willing to admit its relationship to ideology may be a bit less defensive about our mythologic function, but that is no guarantee we will always be conscious of it.

Myths and rituals of women's initiation

Paradoxically, despite Jane Harrison's belief that matrilineal practices had preceded and could still be glimpsed in classical Greek religion, she had little to say about women's initiation. This may be because she was herself the product of an androcentric tradition, or perhaps because she saw men's initiation as more problematic: they were the ones who at adolescence had to break decisively with their mothers and be ritually 'reborn' from males. The more recent myth-and-ritual research has maintained this interest in male initiation, but since the 1970s scholars have also begun to look for traces of female initiation rites in classical myths. Because the evidence for women's actual ritual practices is so slight, there is still disagreement about whether specific rites were meant to be initiatory and about the number of girls in ancient Greece who took part in them. Sometimes there is an explicit connection between a myth or myths and a specific rite; more often, a plot common to several myths is interpreted as reflecting a ritual pattern.[22]

Because initiation has a strong socializing function, girls' rites are usually seen as inculcating the subordinate roles women were expected to assume. Some feminist studies, however, use comparative anthropology to suggest that *women's* understanding of their roles may have been quite different from men's, and that the symbolism found in rites and myths of initiation can be ambiguous or even subversive. The content of the few surviving fragments of poetry by women strongly suggests that there was a 'women's culture' in ancient Greece and Rome. If so, one of its central features must have been women's shared understandings of the rituals they performed together – often in the absence of men.[23] A further possibility, not incompatible with the existence of a women's culture, is that a world view in which religious meanings and practices are central will assign a higher value to religious roles than does the secularized culture of the modern West. Women's lack of political power, in this view, would not be tantamount to their lack of value in the wider scheme of things. Thus the classicist Bella Zweig (now Bella Vivante) has used the model of Native American belief systems to argue for a higher estimate of Greek, and especially Spartan, women's value to their communities.[24]

One of the most intriguing and elusive of women's rituals, from a modern perspective, is the *arkteia* or 'bear-service' performed by young Athenian girls for the goddess Artemis at Brauron and Munichia in Attica. The range of the girls' ages is still debated, but they were all unmarried and some apparently as young as five. In what sense did they 'act the bear' (the Greek verb is *arkteuein*) for Artemis? While some *adults* are portrayed wearing bear-masks in the vase fragments from Brauron, the girls do not dress as bears; they are shown racing, sometimes in the nude, and dancing or walking in procession. The ages of the girls and their activities suggest some form of initiation rite. One of our few written sources (Pausanias, second century CE) claims that all girls had to 'act the bear' before marriage. Yet the sanctuary was not large enough to house the hundreds of girls that such a practice would have involved each year.

Even stranger are the myths told in connection with the rite. At Brauron, it was said that a tame bear, sacred to Artemis, once scratched a girl who had teased it. When the girl's brothers killed the bear in retaliation, a plague struck Athens. Consulting an oracle, the Athenians were told that the plague would be lifted only if their daughters performed the *arkteia*. A variant of this myth, told at Munichia, involved a harsher penalty: one father had to be willing to sacrifice his daughter to the goddess. A clever man named Embaros offered to do so, but dressed a goat in his daughter's clothes and sacrificed it while hiding the girl herself in the inner room of the temple.

These look like aetiological myths, that is, myths told to account for the origin or cause of a practice. But as Ken Dowden has pointed out, we do not have enough information to say which came first, the myth or the rite.[25] Nor does there seem to be a close correspondence between the events of the myth and the actions of the rite. Further, some myths not expressly linked to rites have a similar structure: to remove a plague or other danger threatening an entire community, one girl must be sacrificed. The girl is always of marriageable age but still unmarried. Sometimes she is actually killed; sometimes an animal is substituted for her, and sometimes she herself becomes an animal. If she survives, she may become a priestess (like Iphigeneia, whose tomb was said to be at Brauron) or the mother of a hero (like Io).

Dowden's book, *Death and the Maiden*, identifies a large number of myths with similar plots, which he thinks reflect a widespread practice of girls' initiation in prehistoric Greece.[26] The heroine of the myth, whose supposed tomb was sometimes the site of the ritual, served as 'prototype' for the many girls who underwent the rite. In this view, death and transformation in the myths are essentially metaphors for the social transformation associated with the rite. As in tribal societies that still practice initiation today, the girl's experience might be a true ordeal like that of the mythic heroine, involving sudden separation from her family, isolation from her community, and testing of her skill and stamina (in, e.g., the dances or races shown on the vases). At the end of the segregation period, she and her age-mates would rejoin the community in a new role, as adult women eligible for marriage. In the 'liminal' (threshold) period outside ordinary social structures, the initiates were allowed and even required to act in 'uncivilized' ways, or in ways antithetical to their eventual adult roles. Thus at Brauron, for example, the 'little bears' would have been encouraged to identify with the wildness and ferocity of the bear before relinquishing that side of themselves forever.

To Dowden, the rite explains the basic structure of the myths; but he admits that 'myths ... are stories, and good stories have a life of their own' (*The Uses of Greek Mythology*, 105). Thus – as in Jane Harrison's account – they could become 'detached' from ritual and assume complex new forms in panhellenic epic and Attic tragedy. This explains the fact that the myths exist in so many versions, and that so many details of the myths are not reflected in the rites.

Yet as in the work of Harrison and Burkert, the problem remains: why should initiation be so closely linked – even, in myth, equated – with sacrifice? In particular, why should sacrifice be so prominent in myths associated with *women's* initiation? True, there are myths in which young men are killed at the verge of adulthood: Hippolytos, Hyakinthos, and Adonis are just a few examples. Yet the number of those said to have been ritually *sacrificed* is small by comparison with the number of girls. Surprisingly few interpreters have tackled this question. Burkert, from a self-consciously masculine perspective, argues that the sacrifice of a virgin is the ultimate form of (masculine) renunciation of sex. Helen King has pointed out that in Greek medical writings, the normal flow of women's menstrual blood is compared with the blood of sacrificed animals; like the animals, women are 'bound to bleed', in contrast to the men who alone may draw the blood of *others* in war and sacrifice.[27]

I would argue that in an important sense, women in ancient Greece and Rome were all destined for 'sacrifice', beginning precisely at puberty. I refer not only to the bloodshed of menstruation, defloration and childbirth, or to the dangers inherent in childbirth – dangers augmented by early marriage which virtually guaranteed

3. Myth and Ritual

'teen pregnancy'. The greater, if unspoken, sacrifice women were asked to make was the subordination of all their actual and potential abilities to their marital and reproductive functions. I do not mean to suggest that these women did nothing in adult life but have intercourse and give birth. Rather, their adult lives were organized around these functions, and any activities that were thought to interfere with them – including, in Athens, moving freely about the city – were taboo. Of course young men were asked to risk their lives in battle, and to devote a certain number of years to preparation for this role; but a risk is not the same as a sacrifice, from which escape is impossible. Men, moreover, were rewarded for their risk with full membership in the civic community, while women remained legal minors and had no political rights. In this context, I submit, it made sense to equate women's initiation with sacrifice. The ancient authors never make this connection, so my point is speculative; but one of the functions of myth is to disguise its own ideological effects, so I do not find it surprising that this point is never spelled out.

Helene Foley has described in some detail the parallels between marriage and sacrifice:

> Both rites involve a voluntary death, real or symbolic, designed to ensure social survival. Both seek to gain a propitious future through violence, loss and submission to a social order. Participation in a sacrifice signifies membership in a society and, by implication, submission to its rules and requirements and an entitlement to share in its benefits. Marriage requires a comparable incorporation into the social order.[28]

Notice that the first two of these points focus on the bride: only for her is marriage symbolically equated with death, because only for her is it thought to involve 'violence, loss and submission'. The third point concerns the groom, who by participating in sacrifice – not *being* sacrificed – gains 'membership in a society' and 'entitlement to share in its benefits'. He too must 'submit' to the rules of society, but for him the benefits are obvious, while for the woman they are much less so.

To return to the 'little bears' and related myths, what does it mean in this context for young girls to 'act the bear' for a virgin goddess who is also a hunter? What is their relationship to this fiercely independent goddess – are they merely her victims (like Iphigeneia, or the girl in the myth of Embaros), or are they identified with her in any way?

The related myth of Kallisto offers another approach to this question. Kallisto was not formally associated with a cult of Artemis, but her story invites comparison both with the rites at Brauron and with the myths of maiden sacrifice to Artemis.[29] Kallisto was a member of Artemis' band of maidens, a band who hunted together and shunned all contact with males – in Dowden's words, 'a segregated group between girlhood and womanhood, which in real life is the initiatory group, making the passage from one to the other in seclusion' (*Death and the Maiden*, 190). Kallisto was raped or seduced by Zeus (who in one comic version disguised himself as Artemis to get close to the girl) and became pregnant. She succeeded in hiding her condition until one day she was compelled by the others to strip and bathe. From this point the different versions of the myth diverge widely, but in nearly all of them Kallisto is transformed into a bear (by Artemis or Hera), gives birth to a son Arkas, and is hunted and killed or further transformed into the constellation of the Great Bear.

Dowden has no qualms about equating Kallisto's transformation with the 'bear-service' of Greek girls, because it can be seen as a transitional ('liminal') state that begins when she is stripped of her clothes, and because it culminates in the birth of a child, which 'makes her definitively a woman' (191). But this is to ignore some important features of the myth. Kallisto becomes a bear only when she *leaves* the company of Artemis under duress, and she is never reintegrated into society; in fact, she never even resumes her human form. Hers is not a normal initiation but a failed one – a tragic story of premarital rape and premature death.

Less tragic in its outcome but no less traumatic is the tale of Io, who like Kallisto is forced into a sexual encounter with Zeus, then transformed into an animal – in her case, a cow. Hounded by a monstrous herdsman and a gadfly, both sent by Hera, she is driven literally to the ends of the earth before finding a home in Egypt, where she regains her human shape and gives birth to Zeus' son Epaphos. Her story too has been equated with initiatory ritual because of her expulsion from the community and her wanderings in the wilderness. But as Phyllis Katz has noted, her physical and mental sufferings, as described in Aeschylus' *Prometheus Bound*, may also reflect a distinctive trauma of young girls recorded in the Greek medical writers.[30] A medical treatise *On the Diseases of Unmarried Girls (Peri Partheniôn)* describes a syndrome in which adolescent girls experience suffocation, fevers, hallucinations, and suicidal impulses. The diagnosis is that a girl's womb, empty but driven to procreate, 'wanders' about her body – like the distraught Io – and strikes her heart and lungs. The prescription: to marry and become pregnant as soon as possible. Once heavy with child, the womb will stay in place. Greek medical thought was not systematized or recorded in writing before the classical period, and we cannot say whether this syndrome was confined to that period, but it is easy to see such a trauma arising in a culture that dictated a girl's future and imposed it on her in adolescence. Helen King has shown that the suffocation experienced by the girls, and their efforts to commit suicide by hanging, are paralleled in the epithet 'strangled' given to Artemis herself. For paradoxically, the goddess who presides over girls' transition to adulthood never makes the transition herself: she is a perpetual virgin. Refusing that transition and its 'sacrificial' bleeding, the girls choose a bloodless death by hanging.

From where we stand, millennia later, Artemis is a thoroughly paradoxical figure. To some extent, this can be explained by a contrast between her portrayals in myth and her functions in ritual. Thus in myth she demands the sacrifice of a girl, while in ritual she helps girls move into adulthood. Yet if we look closer, the paradoxes remain in both realms. In the myth of Iphigeneia and the founding myth of Munichia, Artemis demands the death of a girl in exchange for that of an animal – in some versions, because she 'cares for' the animal. Yet she is herself a hunter of animals. And again in some versions, she substitutes yet another animal for the doomed girl, rescuing her at the last moment. In ritual, she presides over practices that seem designed to reconcile girls to their 'domesticated' status as wives and mothers. Yet these rites seem to include an indulgence in 'wildness' – however the girls may have actually 'played the bear', they were symbolically identified with a potentially fierce and rarely domesticated animal.

One possibility, suggested by Paula Perlman, is that the Greeks thought of the bear as a maternal figure whose protectiveness of its cubs was a positive example for human girls.[31] Aristotle's description of the bear, which may reflect older Greek attitudes and beliefs about the animal, emphasizes its maternal instincts and its reproductive cycle. Aristotle believed the bear gave birth during hibernation to unformed cubs whom she had to lick into shape before leading them out of her cave in the spring. The process of hibernation, Perlman argues, is a perfect analogy for 'the ritual pattern of withdrawal, transformation, and return'; the fact that for the bear hibernation corresponds with pregnancy makes her an even better model for 'the transformation from maiden to mother' (122-3).[32]

Yet another perspective on the fierceness of Artemis is offered by Mary Zeiss Stange, a feminist scholar who is not a classicist – but who does hunt, on foot and in wild country.[33] In her view, modern Western urbanites romanticize the wilderness because they are alienated from it. For a hunter, by contrast – a serious one, who knows the land and its creatures intimately – the paradoxes associated with Artemis are part of the fabric of life. Like Bella Zweig, Stange cites Native American beliefs about the interconnectedness of the divine, human, and animal realms as a modern parallel for the ancient worldview we cannot recover. In this perspective, human hunters are not the only predators in the food chain and cannot afford to objectify their prey – indeed, they tend to identify with it, respect it, and even mourn for it. Yet Stange also shares the exhilaration of the chase conveyed by many representations of Artemis and her Roman counterpart Diana. Successful hunting requires physical stamina and mental alertness, and like other athletic pursuits it fosters self-confidence. Stange thinks the elimination of 'woman the hunter' from the 'hunting hypothesis' is part of a much larger pattern in the history of patriarchy, in which women's aggressive impulses and physical aptitudes are denied and repressed to keep women in their place. The women of Greece and Rome were already subject to this denial, but the figure of Artemis, 'a vestige of hunter-gatherer sensibility', was still part of their mythic and ritual repertoire. Stange goes so far as to imagine Artemis '[whispering] to her little she-bears that they, too, are wild nature' (149).

The 'cruelty' of Artemis can be explained in yet another way, not incompatible with this. Herself a virgin, she 'punishes' girls who like Kallisto lose their virginity, though the girls themselves did not seek and could not avoid the sexual encounter. She also 'kills' women in childbirth – or 'saves' them if they survive. In the case of unmarried girls, this could be seen as an enforcement of the patriarchal taboo on intercourse outside of marriage. Yet of the real, as opposed to mythic, women Artemis was said to 'kill', most were surely married. In a culture where death in childbirth was common, it might well seem to be the 'penalty' for losing one's virginity, inflicted by the goddess whose power was linked to an inviolability denied human women.

It is important to admit that we will never know in any detail what ancient women thought and felt about the goddesses they worshipped. It is also important to distinguish between what we *can* know with some probability and what we imagine when we drop the constraints of traditional standards of proof. But imagination is not irrelevant to the scholar. I am interested in Stange's view of Artemis, and in *Xena: Warrior Princess*, because these are figures poised between past and future. They insist in a very unladylike way on the need for changes in our ways of representing women. Yet they also insist on including the past in their vision. This is because the past is precedent and ideal, model and matrix. Thus I turn next to the interpretation of myth as 'charter' for social systems and the attitudes that maintain them.

4

Myth as 'Charter'

As our ancestors in ancient times did – so do we now.

Tibetan prayer[1]

Myth and scholarship

In this chapter I come to grips with the relationship between myth and scholarship in a more direct way than I have yet done. Both are ways of knowing, and as such they have much in common. Each has an explanatory function, offering reasons for puzzling and contradictory features of the world. Thus each lays claim to a kind of truth. Each tends to link its explanations to an account of origins: things are the way they are because of their history. Yet despite these similarities, for modern Western people there is an implicit conflict between myth and scholarship, best expressed in our use of the word 'falsehood'. 'That's a myth!', we say when we want to discredit a popular opinion with which we disagree. Adopting the model of the so-called hard sciences such as chemistry and physics, which have made such spectacular gains in our time, modern scholarship sets itself an ideal of objectivity, of distance between the knower and the known. Myth, by contrast, encourages an identification between these two. A myth 'belongs' to the people who tell it, and it in turn shapes their sense of who they are. A myth is also unashamedly a *story*, with a plot and characters, whereas scholarly explanations are drier, more impersonal accounts. Myths are easier to learn and remember than most scholarly findings; they are more fun. This contrast was expressed in classical Greek by the distinction between *mythos*, 'story', and *logos*, 'reckoning' or 'account'. The two overlapped in usage but could be used (often tendentiously) to draw a line between traditional lore and emerging forms of rationalistic thought such as philosophy and medicine. Thus the historian

100

4. Myth as 'Charter'

Thucydides sought to discredit his predecessors by claiming that 'the mythic' (*to muthôdes*, 1.21) occupied too great a place in their works.

Despite these important differences, I will argue that there is a kind of continuum between scholarship and myth, which we ignore at our peril. Scholarship, in conjunction with social and political institutions, wields great power in our time, and myth has not lost its power; it has simply assumed new forms. In particular, the two overlap in their social dimensions. Each arises in a specific social and historical context, whose concerns it reflects to some extent. But each has an authoritative function that is also social. Both myth and scholarship tell us, 'That's the way things are.' Myth usually adds, ' – and that's the way they should be': it is explicitly normative. Recent scholarship avoids this kind of overt judgment but is often *implicitly* normative: its descriptions can easily become justifications for the status quo. An example often noted by feminists is the current spate of research on gender differences and the brain. Despite impressive evidence that men's and women's brains are more alike than they are different, funds are being poured into the search for those subtle differences. The reason is obviously social: at a time when women have shown they are capable of virtually every kind of 'masculine' work, there is a tremendous stake in reasserting a residue of difference that can maintain, however shakily, the traditional gendered division of labour, especially the assignment of child care to women.

As this example suggests, scholarship has not only social but political implications: it has a part to play in a society's debates over the directions it should take. I will argue that myth also has a political dimension. Because myth is traditional in its origins, we tend to think of it as unchanging; but as my first chapter showed, no myth exists in just one version. One reason for the plurality of versions is the desire of different groups or individuals to stake their own claims to a story and to infuse it with their visions of the way things ought to be. This is most obvious in an overtly pluralistic society, but evidence of it can be found in more 'traditional' societies, both ancient and modern.

Let me add that I have no desire to dissolve the boundaries

101

between myth and scholarship. Later in the chapter I cite some disastrous examples of the effect of such a dissolution. But it would be irresponsible of a teacher and writer whose subject is myth to deny the similarities between her own activity and that of self-confessed mythmakers.

Myth as charter

The idea that myths function as 'charters' or overt justifications for social practices originated with the Polish-born British social anthropologist Bronislaw Malinowski in the 1920s. Malinowski was a 'functionalist' who looked at society as an organism or even a machine whose institutions were the organs or parts that kept it working. Although the extreme brand of functionalism he came to advocate would not be acceptable to most of the scholars discussed in this chapter, his notion of myth as a 'charter' – a public declaration of legitimacy – for social norms and practices is still widespread and useful. Even the structuralists, to whom Malinowski's work surely looks simplistic, can be seen as elaborating on his basic position that myths 'do' something essential in – and for – the society that produces them. In Malinowski's words, 'myth expresses, enhances and codifies belief; it safeguards and enforces morality; it vouches for the efficiency of ritual and contains practical rules for the guidance of man.'[2] (The generic masculine in that formula is a reminder of the androcentric focus of early social science, which still exerts a lingering effect in most of its branches.) Although his early work assumes a distinction between the thought of 'primitive' and more complex societies, Malinowski's essays of the 1930s argue that modern people, whatever their technological or scientific sophistication, cannot do without myth.

Malinowski was not a classicist, and his 'charter' terminology has not been widely adopted by classicists.[3] I use it here because it seems to fit a number of twentieth-century approaches to the interpretation of mythology. Different as they are, these approaches share a concern with origin myths and with their authoritative status – their power to reflect and legitimate the status quo in the culture that produces them. Mircea Eliade and Bruce Lincoln, historians of religion, argue that both myth and ritual draw their power from their claim to repeat the founding acts of creator gods or culture heroes at the dawn of time. A group of 'spiritual feminists' has articulated a vision of early human history that can provide a precedent for gender equality. This approach is usually dismissed by scholars when they take notice of it at all; yet it deserves serious study as a self-conscious example of modern mythmaking. Indo-European comparative mythology, born of linguistics, tries to identify common themes and social divisions in the myths and rituals of the Indo-European cultures, whose languages derive from a common 'parent' language. Considered together, these approaches reveal much about the power of origins – or perceived origins – to shape social reality.

The Romanian-born American scholar Mircea Eliade would have resisted vigorously my attempt to compare him with Malinowski or with anyone who sought to 'reduce' religious life to social life. One of the twentieth century's most influential thinkers on myth, he helped to create the discipline we call 'history of religions' and insisted throughout his long career that religion was *sui generis*, a unique human phenomenon. The religious human being, *homo religiosus* – a category that includes virtually all members of traditional socie-ties, where there is only a single religious tradition – divides the things of this world, including space and time, into sacred and profane, revering as sacred those things that provide a connection to the ultimate reality of the supernatural. Ritual, in Eliade's view, is a re-enactment and in fact a re-*living* of founding events, in which the participants enter sacred time and experience the presence of the gods. Myth has the related function of allowing believers to relive these founding events as they retell them. In Eliade's words,

Myth narrates a sacred history; it relates an event that took place in primordial Time, the fabled time of the 'beginnings'. In other words, myth tells how, through the deeds of Supernatu-ral Beings, a reality came into existence, be it the whole of reality, the Cosmos, or only a fragment of reality – an island, a species of plant, a particular kind of human behavior, an institution. Myth, then, is always an account of a 'creation'; it relates how something was produced, began to *be*. Myth tells only of that which *really* happened, which manifested itself completely.[4]

Though trained as an Indologist – a specialist in Indian texts and cultures – Eliade drew examples from many religious traditions and believed that there were fundamental similiarites among all forms of religion. He even identified a religious kernel in apparently secular modern phenomena such as organized sports and adulation for mass-media heroes.

Clearly, Eliade saw myth as a 'charter' – a precedent and a justification – for *religious* practices. And I believe he was correct in insisting that religion deserves to be recognized as more than a disguised social function. Yet to deny that it *has* social functions would be equally misleading. Beliefs shared by a whole society are necessarily social, at least in part. If myth and ritual are seen as links to the ultimate reality, they can have enormous coercive power. Feminists have been aware of this power from the earliest days of their movement: thus Elizabeth Cady Stanton, an American pioneer of women's political rights, also produced *The Woman's Bible* (1895-98), a commentary on the Hebrew and Christian scriptures, in an attempt to counter the patriarchal effects of traditional Christian theology. More recent women theologians have continued to wrestle with these effects and to produce new translations and interpretations of scripture that recognize a more central place for women in 'salvation history'.[5]

The 'charter' approaches I consider here have in common a concern with the relationship between myth and history. All are intent on elucidating this relationship, either by claiming a historical basis for the details of myth or by showing how myth invokes history as a guarantee of its truth. I believe this focus on the historical status of myth has at least two roots in the culture of the modern West: the Judaeo-Christian belief that God has intervened in history and the strong historical component in our conception of the sciences. Most Jews and Christians have always insisted on the historical reality of at least some details in their foundation stories: the Exodus from Egypt, the death and resurrection of Christ. Likewise, the modern sciences emphasize the historical origins and 'evolution' of the universe, of life on Earth, of social and political sytems. So it is not surprising that some of our most passionate debates about the meaning and uses of mythology should involve its historical basis.

In the late twentieth century, however, scholars in many fields rejected evolutionary or 'diachronic' studies – which look at the development of a phenomenon over time – in favour of 'synchronic' forms of analysis – those that look at 'snapshots' of a problem in limited portions of time. In part, this was in reaction to the evolutionary schemes of earlier scholarship, which now look simplistic: for example, the efforts of early anthropologists to establish definite phases of development through which all cultures must pass, as if a culture were like an organism in its growth from conception to maturity and death. The evolutionary model of scholarly explanation has also been undercut by scientific discoveries that reveal the arbitrary nature of biological evolution itself. These developments have made scholars less willing to frame 'stories' about their data or to fit those data into any type of global explanation. Yet most people seem to need or want a story framework to help them make sense of the world. Hence the continuing struggle over the boundaries between myth and scholarship.

'Charter' approaches have an ambivalent relationship to ideology and to politics, the struggle to forge and refine power relations in the 'real world'. On the one hand, charter approaches can reveal the ideological implications of myth by pointing to its use as a precedent for social norms and practices. On the other hand – as the example of Eliade suggests – a charter approach may work to obscure these same implications by focusing on stable, traditional societies where norms can seem immutable (at least to outsiders). As a corrective, I conclude this chapter with a look at the work of Bruce Lincoln, a student of Eliade who has paid explicit attention to the politics of myth and in so doing has found diversity and change in ostensibly traditional cultures.

A highly influential strand of modern theory that has some qualities of a 'charter' approach is Marxist theory. Though often treated with suspicion because of its connection to a political movement that has had some disastrous outcomes, Marxist thought has had the merit of making explicit the political implications that other approaches tend to conceal. In particular, it has provided a crucial analysis of the workings of ideology – the ways in which forms of thought sustain and reproduce social systems. (Like Freud, Marx and his followers have been more successful in their diagnoses of modern ills than in their prescriptions for relief.) Clearly, myth can be seen as a component of ideology. The earlier forms of Marxist thought saw myth as a simple reflection and justification of the unequal relations between social classes, which in turn were rooted in economics: the relations of each class to the means of production. In later, more nuanced forms, the Marxist analysis of ideology has contributed to the poststructuralist approaches described in Chapter 5. Marxist thought is far from being inherently feminist, but it shares with feminist theory an explicitly political concern: to expose and combat what it perceives as social injustice.[6]

The paradox of charter approaches to the *interpretation* of myth is that they tend to become charter myths themselves – by which I mean not falsehoods but articles of faith, foundation narratives that are central to the world views of those who tell them. Is this because scholarship has not advanced far enough and is still mired in 'magical thinking'? Or is it because myth is necessary to us, a source of meaning that scientific scholarship cannot replace? I will begin with a modern charter approach that looks 'mythic' to most mainstream scholars, the better to identify both the value and the dangers of such an approach.

A modern charter myth

I am Pandora, Giver of All Gifts. She lifted the lid from the large jar. From it She took a pomegranate, which became an apple, which became a lemon, which became a pear. *I bring you flowering trees that bear fruit, gnarled trees hung with olives and this, the grapevine that will sustain you.* She reached into the jar for a handful of seeds and sprinkled them over the hillside. *I bring you plants for hunger and illness, for weaving and dyeing. Hidden beneath My surface you will find minerals, ore, and clay of endless form.* She took from the jar two flat stones. *Attend with care My plainest gift: I bring you flint.*

Then Pandora turned the jar on its side, inundating the hillside with Her flowing grace.

Charlene Spretnak, 'The Myth of Pandora'[7]

Together or alone we dance Her Dance,
We do the work of The Mother,
She we have called Goddess for human comprehension.
She, the Source, never-to-be grasped Mystery,
Terrible Cauldron, Womb,
Spinning out of her the unimaginably small
And the immeasurably vast –
Galaxies, worlds, flaming suns –
And our Earth, fertile with her beneficence,
Here, offering tenderest flowers.
(Yet flowers whose roots may split rock.) ...

Thus is She
And being of Her
Thus am I.
Powered by Her,
As she gives, I may give,
Even of my blood and breath:
But none may require it;
And none may question me.

I am.
I am That I am.

Elsa Gidlow, 'A Creed for Free Women'[8]

Elsa Gidlow deliberately uses the language of biblical monotheism to invoke a Goddess who can be seen as the equal of the biblical God in 'His' self-sufficiency and unquestioned authority. At the same time, Gidlow uses the language of modern science to describe the forces at work in nature, at both microscopic and telescopic levels – forces that despite our progress in mapping them remain 'mysterious'. We invoke the Goddess, says Gidlow, 'for human comprehension'. This is one of the most explicit and self-conscious statements of what I will call the 'charter myth' of the feminist spirituality movement: a belief in ancient and abiding representations of the divine as female, which in turn confer power on human women. This belief takes many forms: to some, it is the equivalent of belief in the traditional God of the Bible; to others, a deliberate personification of natural forces or a projection of Jungian archetypes (as discussed in Chapter 2). It is the belief of a distinct minority, a grass-roots movement of well-educated American and European women (most of them white) who come together in small groups for workshops and rituals but who shun organization on a larger scale.[9] Through journals, books, and websites, their beliefs have reached a wider audience and have even been mentioned in textbooks. Yet the heat of the debate they have generated seems out of all proportion to their influence in society at large. Ironically, they have been castigated most vigorously by feminist archaeologists, classicists, and historians of religion for taking a utopian view of the past and a reductive, 'essentialist' view of women's capacities. As I did in the case of Jungian uses of goddess mythology, I will consider the dangers of essentialism while insisting on the power these representations hold for a considerable number of contemporary women.

What is the 'charter myth' of the feminist spirituality movement? Briefly, it is the belief that goddess worship was once universal or nearly so, and that this form of religion both reflected and inspired social arrangements in which women were the equals, if not the rulers, of men. In particular, matriliny, the practice of tracing descent from the mother (rather than from the father, as in patriliny), is thought to have ensured the high status of women as well as their power to control property and to make important decisions. Since the chief deities were female, women who served them as priestesses were seen as sharing their power. In the 'Goddess charter' view, cultures where goddess worship went hand in hand with women's authority were peaceful and egalitarian, sharing rather than hoarding resources and lacking any motive to make war. This state of affairs came to an end, in Europe at least, with the invasion of the Indo-Europeans, a nomadic and patrilineal people who imposed their language, their male gods, and their patriarchal ideology on the peoples they conquered.

Anyone who doubts the intellectual and moral seriousness of the issues raised by the Goddess movement should read Carol Christ's *Laughter of Aphrodite*.[10] Christ is an academic, trained in theology and religious studies, who after a long and painful struggle decided she could no longer accept the Judaeo-Christian vision of God – a God who has been invoked to justify not only the antisemitism that culminated in the Holocaust but 'the oppression of women through-out patriarchal history' (6). In the process of writing her dissertation on the novels of Elie Wiesel, Christ 'came to agree with Wiesel that either God is not just or he is not powerful'. But she did not conclude that all forms of divinity are mere human projections. Gradually she turned to the worship of a Goddess whom she understands as both one and many. The most specific manifestations of the Goddess described in her book are Greek – Demeter, Persephone, and above all Aphrodite. Writing near the end of the Cold War, Christ ended her book with a powerful and articulate critique of the mind/body dualism in Western thought that in her view has sustained both the arms race and the subordination of women. Beginning with Plato, many Western philosophers have posited a split between mind and body that includes what Christ calls a 'denial of finitude' – an insistence on the ability of mind or spirit to transcend the limita-tions of the body. By contrast, she sees the Goddess(es) as a form of divinity that is immanent in the natural world, not 'above' and separate from it. They enable her to imagine and practise 'a spiritu-ality that acknowledges finitude and death and that encourages us to affirm rather than deny our connections with the earth' (222). Not content merely to re-read the story of Demeter and Persephone, Christ retells it at Eleusis as part of a ritual in which women also share their own stories of alienation from and reunion with mothers and daughters. She admits that some elements of her rituals resem-ble modern forms of psychotherapy (106). But in contrast to Jungian therapists who use the goddesses as names for archetypes, Christ insists on their external reality and always capitalizes the word Goddess – which, she notes, 'still remains unspeakable even to many of the most radical Christian and Jewish [feminist] theologians'. It

109

is taboo, she argues, because to identify female power with the divine is still profoundly 'threatening to the status quo' (111).

The literature of the Goddess movement has been an easy target for scholars because most of its authors, unlike Christ, are non-academics who lack a sense of complexity and nuance in the interpretation of ancient evidence. Yet a classicist reading a book like Charlene Spretnak's *Lost Goddesses of Early Greece* cannot help but be struck by the fact that most of the authorities she cites are classicists. True, they are classicists of an earlier time: Jane Harrison, Lewis Farnell, George Thomson. But if their methodologies have been superseded, their grasp of complexity and nuance cannot be impugned. The major difference between them and contemporary classicists is their reliance on evolutionary schemas, from which a story is more easily generated than from the more fragmentary synchronic ('snapshot') studies of today. The general public has not stopped looking to the past for origins and precedents. It may be that in our rejection of evolutionary models we have unwittingly created an interpretive gap – one which the 'Goddess charter' aspires to fill.

The evidence brought forward in support of the 'Goddess charter myth' is of two kinds: archaeological and mythological. Although they overlap, I will discuss them separately because they are usually studied by separate groups of scholars.

Archaeology: sites of struggle

In the archaeological record, a major category of evidence consists of the clay figurines found in many Neolithic ('new stone age') sites in Europe. Because they are made of durable material, they have survived in fairly large numbers. For a period that left no written records, they provide precious if limited evidence for belief systems. It used to be said by most scholars that a large majority of these figurines have female traits, such as enlarged breasts or hips and clearly indicated pubic triangles. Recent 'recounts' have found higher numbers of male traits and a large percentage of figures displaying either no sexual characteristics or a combination of male and female traits.[11] It has also been pointed out that while the figurines were produced over an enormous span of time – some as

110

early as the Palaeolithic ('old stone age', up to 26,000 years ago) –
there are many periods and places in which they are lacking. While
the traditional assumption was that these figurines had some form
of ritual use, recent academic studies are more and more hesitant to
identify them with goddesses.

Other aspects of the archaeological record that are important to
the 'Goddess charter' are the presence or absence of weapons and
fortifications, and any indications of the distribution of wealth, such
as grave goods, the objects buried with the dead. A particularly
important site for these forms of evidence, as well as for its spectacular plastic art, is the Neolithic mound of Çatalhöyük in Turkey,
originally excavated in the 1960s and re-opened in 1993. Here again,
there is a striking difference of opinion between the original excavator,
James Mellaart – who is often cited in the Goddess literature – and the
new team, led by Ian Hodder. Mellaart painted a clear picture of a
stable, egalitarian community whose burial patterns (children with
mothers, and apart from fathers) strongly suggested matrilineal descent. In Mellaart's account, many rooms are identified as 'shrines' and
the only anthropomorphic deities are said to be female. By contrast, a
recent report by Lynn Meskell on the new excavations rejects not only
Mellaart's conclusions but the accuracy of his data:

> Firstly, in terms of the structures themselves, we cannot sepa-
> rate out shrines and non-shrines ... The boundaries between
> what we would call religious and secular are blurred, and
> perhaps even irrelevant. As for social equality, this too has
> come into question. Burial evidence is certainly uneven, with
> some individuals having differential wealth on the basis of age
> and sex. Data from the earlier excavations has proven to be
> unreliable and so earlier arguments based on the placement of
> male and female burials can only be dubious.[12]

The archaeologist whose name crops up most often in the recent
debates is Marija Gimbutas. She is invariably cited by advocates of
the Goddess charter because she came to embrace it herself in the
last ten years of her life. From a lifelong study of female figurines,
tombs, and 'temples' of Neolithic cultures of the Balkan region

(Bulgaria, Greece, Hungary, and her native Yugoslavia), she arrived at the conviction that goddess worship in these cultures was related to a higher status for women in a peaceful, egalitarian, and environmentally stable form of society.[13] In her view, the cultures of 'Old Europe', which flourished from roughly 7000 to 3000 BCE, were partly destroyed and partly assimilated by the Indo-European invaders, who brought with them a male-dominated pantheon of gods to match their patrilineal and hierarchical social structure. But these views, which make Gimbutas the authority of choice for spiritual feminists, are increasingly under attack by other archaeologists, including most of the small number who identify themselves as feminist. In fact, a survey of recent books on the issue makes it painfully clear that the advent of feminist approaches in archaeology has not led – at least thus far – to a vindication of Mellaart's and Gimbutas' vision of a prehistory in which goddess-worship ensured respect for women.

Archaeologists occupy a special position in the goddess debate because they can legitimately claim that they – in contrast to textual critics – have more and better evidence than was available to earlier generations of classicists. It is a profound irony of scholarship that more evidence often leads to more uncertainty because it makes us aware that what we are studying is more complex than we had thought. I would argue that the sheer amount of information available to contemporary archaeologists makes them hesitant to generalize about the 'big picture' as their predecessors did. But the willingness or unwillingness to describe broad patterns in the evidence and to reach conclusions based on these patterns is also shaped by social and political forces in the culture producing the scholarship. Feminist approaches are still anathema to many archaeologists, including many women archaeologists,[14] so those who wish to espouse them must be especially careful to display the objectivity that is central to the discipline's self-conception. At stake are these women's credentials as archaeologists, their chances of publication and their very jobs. It seems especially important to them to repudiate the conclusions of Gimbutas, the only well-known and (formerly) respected archaeologist to have embraced the Goddess spirituality movement. In the Goddess literature, Gimbutas is

112

universally cited as an authority; in the archaeological literature, article after article, book after book bring her forward as the example to be avoided: the scholar who became a 'true believer' – and thereby ceased to be a scholar.

The most thoughtful writers on both sides of this debate see it explicitly as a boundary dispute between scholarship and mythology. The word 'myth', when it appears, may carry the modern connotation of 'fiction', but it is also understood as part of a belief system. Feminist archaeologists argue that Gimbutas and her followers have forced ambiguous evidence into a simplistic mould to support a charter myth of gender equality. Advocates of Goddess spirituality reply that mainstream scholars are using claims of objectivity to mask an equally mythic assumption of universal male supremacy.

Despite the apparent opposition between these positions, I believe they are in fact quite close; this may even be one reason for the vehemence of the debate. Both sides understand that religion is, at least in part, a social phenomenon: a source of cohesion among people and of models and sanctions for their behaviour. Both also realize that scholarship has some of these same functions. In particular, there is constant give and take in the academy between what the anthropologist Clifford Geertz called the 'model of' and the 'model for': the attempt to describe in faithful detail the culture 'as it is' and the attempt to formulate ideals for its emulation.[15] In an age and a society where the common culture is secular, scholarship comes to carry a large share of the authority that other societies have vested in religion. This authority has both an intellectual and a moral dimension. People look to scholars – most of whom are also teachers – for descriptions of the world and explanations of how it got to be the way it is; but these descriptions are also taken as normative. Those with greater knowledge of 'the way things are' tend to be consulted about 'the way things should be'. As in religion, there is a *consensus* in scholarship; the questions asked, the methods used, even – some would argue – the answers obtained, must fall within acceptable bounds. Scholars whose findings are too discordant with this consensus can find themselves ostracized unless and until they are fortunate enough to bring about conceptual revolutions in their fields. Although critics of the academy sometimes speak as if there were an ideological conspiracy among scholars, the consensus I have described is far more subtle than this. Yet it is naive to assume that scholarship can ever be completely objective, uninfluenced by the norms of the culture that produces it.

For the lay person, mythology has a clear advantage over scholarship: it is easier to understand and (partly for that reason) more enjoyable. It tells a story about characters who are recognizably human, and it has an outcome of some kind. It can be grasped and appreciated as a discrete whole even if it is actually implicated in a much larger system of stories and beliefs. Precisely because it is a clear, accessible whole, it can serve as a charter for an institution or practice that seems otherwise too complex to grasp. Myths are easily told, retold, and passed from one person to another. Scholarship requires years of study, specialized terminology, and a detached stance that can become alienating or merely boring. In this perspective, it is unfair to compare the ease and pleasure of reading a popularizing book such as Riane Eisler's *The Chalice and the Blade,* which is closer to the pole of mythology, with the difficulty of a more scholarly collection such as *Ancient Goddesses: The Myths and the Evidence,* edited by Lucy Goodison and Christine Morris.[16] Goodison, Morris, and their collaborators have 'paid their dues' in years of painstaking research; if anyone has earned the right to speak authoritatively on their subject, they have. The disappointment is that they abdicate this right by avoiding *any* clear conclusions, insisting that the realities are too complex.

In fact, they cite feminist reasons for their refusal to draw definite conclusions. In a chapter on the female figurines that are often cited as primary evidence of goddess worship in prehistory, Ruth Tringham and Margaret Conkey point out that to insist *all* such figurines represent goddesses is to impose a 'totalizing' and authoritarian account of the kind that has characterized traditional androcentric archaeology. A modern understanding of religion and its relation to the rest of a culture may be anachronistic for the periods in which the figurines were produced. At a time when archaeology is just beginning to accept more pluralistic approaches, feminists within the field are suspicious of a unitary account in which goddess-worship sustains a homogeneous culture for millennia.

114

Perhaps their strongest argument is based on the history of scholarship. For the belief in prehistoric 'matriarchy' – a stage of civilization in which women were predominant – originated with male scholars who thought that human progress had meant getting *beyond* that stage. J.J. Bachofen, the Swiss classicist whose book *Mother Right* (*Das Mutterrecht*, 1861) is usually considered the most influential nineteenth-century account of matriarchy, is distant enough from us that we can see clearly how he imposed on the past the ideas about women prevailing in his own era. His matriarch ruled from a 'pedestal' of chastity and moral superiority; her rule was grounded in her 'natural' biological role as a mother, and her political rule ended with the recognition of the 'divine father principle' and the transcendent spirituality it fostered.

There was however a contemporary alternative to Bachofen's charter account of primitive matriarchy. In early Marxist thought, especially in the work of Friedrich Engels, patriarchy was not an ideal but an evil thought to have arisen along with the private ownership of property. In *The Origin of the Family, Private Property, and the State* (1884), Engels argued that the social inequality of women and men had come about at the same time as economic inequality and from the same causes. The Marxist ideal was to eliminate both forms of inequality.

Both Bachofen's and Engels' theories were rooted in an evolutionist model of human society that has since been rejected. Contemporary with the Darwinian theory of biological evolution, it looked for a prescribed sequence of stages in the development of a society, analogous to the stages of development of a living organism.[17] From where we stand, this kind of social theory looks very much like an 'origin myth'. But it is important to recognize that origin myths are not just outmoded science; they have political implications, as does science itself.

The politics of origin myths

Modern critiques of Bachofen emphasize the fact that, living before the advent of scientific archaeology, he depended on classical mythology for his evidence. If mythology had a historical basis, he

115

argued, there must have been a time when women ruled: didn't Hesiod describe a primordial female, Gaia, as the first parent, who was stripped of her preeminence by a series of male gods? Didn't Apollo establish his oracle at Delphi by defeating an earlier female occupant of the site? On the human plane, Clytemnestra, wife of Agamemnon, loses power and credibility in a series of struggles with males: though she succeeds in ruling a kingdom in the absence of her husband and kills him on his return from Troy for having sacrificed their daughter Iphigeneia, she is killed in turn by her son Orestes. Orestes is then acquitted on the grounds that it was his sacred duty to avenge his father, even if it meant killing his mother, since the father is the 'true parent'. In Aeschylus' *Oresteia* trilogy, the best-known and most culturally prestigious version of this myth, the last act is a showdown between younger male gods (Apollo and Zeus), who support Orestes, and older female gods (the Erinyes or Furies), who support Clytemnestra. The victory of the males is sealed by the female, but male-identified, Athena, who breaks a tied vote in favour of Orestes and reconciles the Furies to a subordinate but 'honoured' position in Zeus' new regime.

A parallel but less familiar myth, retold by the early Christian philosopher Augustine,[18] describes a contest between Athena and Poseidon for the patronage of Athens. The whole population of the city takes part in the vote, which is strictly determined by gender; since women outnumber men by one, the goddess wins. The women themselves lose, however: they are deprived of political rights when Poseidon throws a tantrum at the outcome and floods the city. Ironically, although Athens takes its name from the goddess, the women who ensured her victory are deprived of the very name 'Athenian'.

On a purely mythological basis, then, Bachofen had a strong case – if not for matriarchy in the full sense, then for a period in which women shared power with men. But it is also important to consider the ways in which these stories were framed for the ancient audience. If the Greeks themselves believed there was matriarchy in their past, what was their attitude to it? Was it a lost utopia, or – as for Bachofen – a more primitive state that had been superseded? Surely for Hesiod and Aeschylus (and the Christian Augustine) it was the latter. In a path-breaking article, 'The Dynamics of Misogyny: Myth and Mythmaking in the *Oresteia*', the Hellenist Froma Zeitlin showed how Aeschylus' poetry equated female power with the negative poles of a whole series of oppositions: reason/unreason, light/dark, Greek/'barbarian', order/chaos.[19] Comparing the myths cited by Bachofen with similar stories in non-Western traditions, the anthropologist Joan Bamberger showed (in 1974, even before Zeitlin's article) that such stories are often used explicitly to discredit the 'rule of women', whether or not such rule ever existed in history.[20] The point was that women – or goddesses – abused their rule and were justly deposed. Thus the kinds of stories about women's power in the past that modern women want to use as charter myths for a feminist future have also been used as charters for patriarchy. This does not necessarily make them unusable for feminist purposes, but it does show us that their ideological effects cannot be taken for granted.

Compared to the evidence from archaeology, that from ancient mythology is both more and less clear. It is clearer insofar as it is verbal: instead of nameless figurines, we have clearly identified male and female characters who have specific powers, roles, and relationships. But myths, like archaeological data, pose their own distinctive problems as sources for history. Since the surviving texts were all produced in historical times (indeed, 'historical' times are defined as those from which we have texts), their reliability for earlier ages can always be questioned. Even if they can be shown to descend from a long oral tradition, there is no guarantee that the details of a given version have not been tailored to suit a particular audience in historically specific circumstances. In fact, when an era is well-documented it is often easy to show that this has been done. The tragedies, including the *Oresteia*, which were produced in an age about which we know a great deal from non-mythic sources, can be seen to reflect quite specific social and political debates. The argument over whether the mother or father is the 'true parent', for example, was mirrored in contemporary Greek medical and biological theory, and was linked to the political issue of how to define citizenship in the Athenian democracy.

If, then, the myths cannot be taken as straightforward evidence

117

of what happened in prehistory, they *can* be seen as involved in social and political realities. If they are discounted as 'models *of*' ancient societies – true pictures of the way those societies functioned – they can be taken seriously as 'models *for*' – projections of ideal norms for behaviour and social arrangements. In the next section of this chapter I will consider an influential version of the latter approach: that of the Indo-European comparativists.

Indo-European comparative mythology

A distinctive approach to the social content of myth is that of 'Indo-European comparative mythology', pioneered by the French scholar Georges Dumézil. This approach is rooted in the discovery of nineteenth-century linguists that most of the modern languages spoken in Europe belong to a single family which also includes the Iranian and some Indian languages. Called 'Indo-European' (abbreviated IE), the family includes Latin and its descendants the Romance languages as well as Greek, Sanskrit, Persian, and the Celtic, Germanic, Baltic, and Slavic sub-families. By systematically comparing the grammar and vocabularies of these descendant languages, scholars have worked out a family tree and a sketch of the 'parent' language, called Proto-Indo-European (PIE), which has left no written traces. Since language and culture are so closely intertwined, it seems reasonable to expect that speakers of the Indo-European languages will have some cultural traits and values in common, transmitted along with the languages themselves – and with the traditional oral genres of poetry and folklore. Already in the nineteenth century, scholars were compiling lists of cognate words that suggested some cultural traits could be traced back to the Proto-Indo-Europeans, such as stock breeding, the wheel, and belief in a male sky god. But Georges Dumézil was the first to argue, in the 1930s, that the descendant cultures share 'a common set of myths functionally interrelated to a common set of social institutions, to a common ideology, whether in ancient Italy, Scandinavia, Iran, or even Greece'.[21] ('Even' Greece because Greek myth and religion were heavily influenced by non-IE cultures of the Near East and Crete.) In simplified terms, this ideology is said to have comprised three hierarchically ranked 'functions', corresponding to three idealized social strata: priests, warriors, and 'herder-cultivators'. Dumézil further subdivided the first function into 'magico-religious' and 'juridical-contractual' powers, exercised by priests and kings respectively. In fact, the kings in most of these cultures emerged from the ranks of the warriors but were consecrated or legitimized by the priests. As ruler of the whole society, the king was in a sense outside of any one function and expected to provide for the welfare of all.

In some IE societies, these idealized 'functions' correspond to actual social classes. For example, the Indian caste hierarchy of brahman, ksatriya, and vaisya (priest, warrior, and herder-cultivator), already reflected in the Vedic hymns (second millennium BCE), corresponds to the division of Celtic society into druids, warriors, and 'cow-freemen' (*bo airig*). In other societies the evidence of a 'tripartite ideology' is less direct and comes from ritual or mythology. Thus the Romans appointed three major *flamines* or priests to serve the divine triad of Jupiter, Mars, and Quirinus. Each of these gods is said to represent one of the functions: Jupiter that of the sovereign, Mars that of the warrior, and Quirinus that of the 'producer' or 'progenitor'.[22] Intriguingly, the *flamen dialis*, dedicated to the worship of Jupiter, had to observe a long list of taboos corresponding to those observed by Hindu brahmans. Roman myth, as preserved in ostensibly factual accounts of the founding and early history of Rome, also seems to reflect traces of the Indo-European 'tripartite ideology'. Thus the first king, Romulus, is associated with all three chief gods and all three functions, while each of his successors personifies one function more fully. Numa Pompilius establishes priesthoods and sacred laws; Tullus Hostilius wages war; Ancus Marcius and his successors the Tarquins focus on public works projects and the economy.[23]

As these examples suggest, the ideology that has been reconstructed for the Proto-Indo-Europeans is heavily androcentric. The father is head of each household, and by projection the supreme god is also designated 'father' – hence the parallel names of Greek *Zeus pater* ('father Zeus') and Roman *Iuppiter* (anglicized as Jupiter).[24] Given the role assigned to the Indo-Europeans in the Goddess

119

charter myth, where they bring an end to the peaceful matrilineal culture of Old Europe, it is interesting that specialists in IE comparative mythology seldom address issues of gender in any overt way. This reflects the unselfconscious androcentrism that marked most Western scholarship until very recently. Thus it is possible to read some entire works of Dumézil and his students without encountering any mention of women, as if not just the Indo-European ideology but even its constituent classes were entirely masculine. Even the gods who represent the functions are all male, with the exception of a single 'solar female' associated with the Divine Twins who represent the third function, that of the 'herder-cultivators'. (The Greek Helen, sister of the twin Dioscuri, may be a reminiscence of this goddess, who appears in Indian myth as Surya, daughter of the Sun and bride of the twin Asvins.) Miriam Robbins Dexter, one of the few Indo-Europeanists to tackle gender issues directly, says that on linguistic grounds only four relatively minor goddesses can be identified as of IE origin. All of these are personified forces of nature: the Dawn, the Sun-Maiden, the Earth, and a hazy figure associated with the control and release of waters.[25] Jaan Puhvel claims to have identified one powerful IE goddess he calls 'transfunctional' because her influence extends to all three functions – ruling, warfare, and herding/agriculture.[26] Dexter, however, argues that such 'transfunctional' goddesses – which exist in all the major IE traditions, but lack the cognate names that could securely identify them as IE – are survivals of the goddesses of Old Europe. IE goddesses appear more powerful in the analysis of Wendy Doniger [O'Flaherty], who has found commonalities among Indian, Irish, and Greek myths of sexual and gender conflict.[27] So recognizing IE myths of female power may simply be a matter of looking harder for them. At the same time, it is difficult to deny that most IE traditions as we now know them are heavily androcentric.

Parallels between the vocabulary and grammars of individual IE languages can be extended to the special 'language' of literature. Since the mid-nineteenth century, scholars have recognized that some poetic metres and epic 'formulas' (set phrases) are shared by two or more IE languages, such as Indian and Greek; for example, the Vedic formula *śrávah ... ákṣitam* is equivalent to the Homeric

120

kleos aphthiton, 'immortal fame'). This means that some literary genres and themes can be traced back to a Proto-Indo-European culture.

Few scholars have attempted to catalog these themes, perhaps because some of the specific comparisons are speculative, but a very interesting picture emerges when the attempt is made. Dumézil himself compared the warrior figures of Herakles (Greek), Tullus Hostilius and Horatius (Roman), Indra and Trita Aptya (Indian). In each case the warrior fulfils his chief function of protecting the state and people from enemy attack, but he goes too far, killing members of his own family and requiring purification. There are even parallel stories in which the warrior commits three characteristic 'sins', one against *each* of the three functions, as Herakles (in the version of Diodorus Siculus) opposes the sovereignty of Eurystheus, kills an enemy whose back is turned, and commits adultery (an offence against the third function, which includes human sexuality). Myths like these seem to explore the tension inherent in the warrior's role between protection – his ostensible purpose – and violence – the means of protection, which can so easily be turned against those he is supposed to protect.

Starting from a detailed comparison of oral-traditional formulas, Calvert Watkins argues that PIE culture included the theme of 'hero kills dragon [serpent]'.[28] While he admits that this theme is found in non-IE traditions as well – some of which may have influenced the versions that have come down to us – he identifies IE verbal roots for his proto-formula. He accepts the verdict of earlier scholars that 'the dragon symbolizes Chaos, in the largest sense, and killing the dragon represents the ultimate victory of Cosmic Truth and Order over Chaos' (299). To this basic scenario Watkins adds a wealth of evidence that the *poet*, by preserving the fame of the hero, plays a central role in the transmission of ideology.

It has even been argued that we can identify a PIE creation myth, which like the dragon-slaying myth links creation to an act of killing. The first human, a male who in some versions is also the first king, is sacrificed and dismembered by his twin brother, and the physical world or the social hierarchy – or both – are fashioned from the pieces.[29] In addition to Indic and Germanic versions, the

121

Roman historicized account of Romulus and Remus can be seen to fit this pattern. The name of Remus may even be cognate with the names of Indic Yama and Norse Ymir, which mean 'twin'; each of these figures must die so that something may be created. In the Norse version, the world itself is created from the flesh of the victim. In the Roman case, the creation is that of the city of Rome rather than the world, and there is no dismemberment – though this detail may have been 'surreptitiously preserved' in a curious story about the death of *Romulus*, in which he is murdered and dismembered by the Senate; each senator then takes a piece of the body home with him, concealing it under his toga.[30] Walter Burkert, whose theories about sacrifice I discussed in Chapter 3, has argued that this latter story is a 'mythic sociogony', an account of the origin of society, in which Romulus represents the original totality of the state and the senators represent the families (*gentes*) of which it was composed. Like the historical ritual of the Feriae Latinae, in which a bull was sacrificed and its meat distributed according to strict rules among the various Latin peoples that had been absorbed by Rome, the myth of Romulus' murder by the Senate describes 'the creation of social groupings from the dismembered body of a focal victim'.[31]

One of the few reconstructed PIE myths to involve a female is one in which a king must be raised or restored to the throne through the aid of a virgin. On closer inspection, it is not the virgin herself so much as her procreative power that plays the crucial role: she provides sons who vindicate the deposed king and carry on his line. A Roman example is that of Numitor, who is 'divested of his kingship and restored at long last only after his virginal daughter Rhea Silvia has miraculously conceived and borne the "complete" grandson Romulus, begotten by Mars, having Jupiter as a mentor, and turning into Quirinus'.[32] (Of course, she also bears the ill-starred Remus.) Throughout the history of Rome, long after the deposition of the kings, there were still Vestal Virgins, actual priestesses who by preserving their virginity were believed to preserve the safety of the Roman state. Puhvel describes them as 'symbolic reservoirs of untapped, ripe, stockpiled human potential' (267). He sees several IE parallels to Rhea Silvia: the Indian figure of Madhavi, whose virginity is miraculously restored as she bears a series of sons to different royal husbands; and the two Irish figures named Medb, who confer sovereignty on the series of men they marry. In the latter case, Puhvel argues, there has been 'a perversion of the protomyth' because the Medbs are the dominant figures, choosing their own lovers and punishing them for any signs of sexual jealousy. The IE king, Puhvel asserts, 'needed a virgin to keep him safe and warm, not a browbeating harridan who outranked him and tested his immunity to jealousy' (265). He thinks the Medbs may represent a conflation of the IE virgin with the 'transfunctional goddess', who has the power of conferring sovereignty on the hero she favours.

If the patterns identified by Puhvel, Watkins, and Lincoln are truly representative of the PIE heritage, perhaps spiritual feminists are not so wrong-headed in seeing that heritage as their enemy. Not only are the protagonists of these stories all male, but the central event in nearly every case is an act of killing – even when the killing is paradoxically said to result in creation. What is created, in the dragon-slaying myth or in that of Romulus and Remus, is Order, whether it take the form of a state, a pantheon, or the cosmos itself. The 'tripartite ideology' identified by Dumézil is not just androcentric but strongly hierarchical: priests and kings, at the apex, provide direction, while the warriors enforce their rule and the 'herder-cultivators' produce a surplus to support them. The hierarchy is authorized and sustained by the myths and their associated rituals.

Of course, Proto-Indo-European is a scholarly reconstruction, for which our only evidence is the historical Indo-European cultures: those still extant and those that have left records. The reconstruction is unavoidably shaped by modern ideologies. But in an earlier phase, Indo-European scholarship was also guilty of aiding and abetting one particularly destructive modern ideology: that of racism. Most of those who investigated the IE heritage were themselves Europeans, and quite a few of these assumed the IE peoples shared a racial superiority that accounted for their dominance over other cultural groups. Those who think of the academy as an ivory tower unsullied by politics should take a hard look at the history of scholarly support for racism, including antisemitism, of which the Nazi 'Aryan Myth' is only the best-known instance. As J.P. Mallory puts it, we would be quite mistaken to imagine that this grotesque obsession with the Indo-Europeans or, as they were then more popularly known, the Aryans, was merely the creation of a handful of Nazi fanatics. A fascination with the 'Aryans' was, in fact, very much a part of the intellectual environment of the nineteenth and early twentieth centuries.[33]

I do not mean to suggest that the IE comparative method is necessarily or inherently racist, but rather that scholarship takes place in the 'real world', where it is subject to political influences and can exert such influences in turn. Like myth itself, it can become a 'model for' society, with unexpected and even disastrous results.

Myth and history

If we consider the major monotheistic traditions, which have shaped the religious experience of most people in the modern West, it is not surprising that our approaches to myth put so much emphasis on historical origins. For each of these traditions identifies a series of founding events, which it insists are *historical* events: the exodus from Egypt, the death and resurrection of Christ. The scarcity of external evidence for these events – that is, evidence from outside the religious tradition itself – is no deterrent to the belief in their historical reality. This is because the intervention of God in the history of 'His' people is a central tenet of each faith. Moreover, key rituals in each tradition – the Passover Seder, the Easter service – include retellings of the *stories* of these events, designed to bring them alive for generations that could not have witnessed them. In the words of the traditional Seder, 'In every generation, every Jew must feel as if he himself came out of Egypt'.

This brings us back to Mircea Eliade's view that all myths are essentially charters, in the sense of precedents for subsequent behaviour. He quotes the words of a Tibetan prayer: 'As our ancestors in ancient times did – so do we now'. It is easy to see how this view of myth could be seen as inherently conservative, even reactionary.[34] If there is only one primordial model for human behaviour, how can change be validated? To change our ways, must we change our myths? But the notion of self-consciously changing our myths seems contradictory given the emphasis on what Eliade calls their 'reality'. I believe this is why the Goddess charter myth is so attractive: it claims a historical basis. There *was* a time, it insists – before the arrival of the upstart male gods – when women were respected because goddesses were powerful.

Bruce Lincoln, a student and colleague of Eliade at the University of Chicago, has taken Eliade's theory in a new and promising direction. Using concrete examples from the recent past, for which we have ample evidence, he shows that the charter function of myth is not incompatible with social and political change. As soon as we look closely at a living tradition, we are reminded that it is normal for myths to exist in multiple competing versions, which represent different voices and positions within the parent culture.[35] The success of a version at any given time will depend on its adherents' ability to mobilize a following. Thus myth is not inherently unitary and static but plural and dynamic. For example, if two peoples think of themselves as descended from two brothers, they can choose to emphasize their differences by invoking one of the brothers as ancestor; or they can emphasize their kinship by invoking their common ancestor, the father of both brothers. Jews and Arabs, for example, can invoke their separate descent from Isaac and Ishmael, or their joint descent from Abraham. The ancient Athenians and Spartans, who spoke Ionic and Doric dialects respectively, could invoke the separate ancestors Ion and Doros or their common grandfather Hellen, father of all the 'Hellenes'.[36]

Lincoln's study is especially useful because side by side with examples that most Westerners consider 'mythic' it considers the use of documented historical events as charters. Lincoln emphasizes that it is not the 'fact' of the original event but its repeated *invocation* that endows it with mythic power. More than one founding event (historic or fictional) might be chosen as the basis of a group's identity, and there is significance in choosing one over another – the American Civil War, for example, as opposed to the Revolutionary War. It is obvious at our moment in history that charter myths can have divisive and violent effects: witness the invocation of the Battle of Kosovo to justify the 'ethnic cleansing' of Bosnia in the 1990s, or the biblical model of a 'Greater Israel' used by some Israelis to oppose any accommodation with the Palestinians. But not all conflict is destructive; we should recall that some forms of it, such as labour and civil rights movements, can be seen – at least in retrospect – to have highly positive effects.

I believe that Lincoln's model of the dynamics of myth is also relevant to the struggles I have described between archaeologists and spiritual feminists, or between the conflicting accounts of human evolution discussed in Chapter 3. Knowledge itself is neither static nor unified, but for this very reason we cling to charter narratives that can offer us a sense of purpose and identity, 'a local habitation and a name' in the flux of history. In Lincoln's words,

> To hold that thought is socially determined does not mean that all thought reflects, encodes, re-presents, or helps replicate the established structures of society, for society is far broader and more complex than its official structures and institutions alone. Rather, such a formulation rightly implies that all the tensions, contradictions, superficial stability, and potential fluidity of any given society as a whole are present within the full range of thought and discourse that circulates at any given moment. Change comes not when groups or individuals use 'knowledge' to challenge ideological mystification, but rather when they employ thought and discourse, including even such modes as myth and ritual, as effective instruments of struggle.[37]

This more complex view of the relationship between myth and scholarship, in which both participate in something called *discourse*, will be explored further in the next chapter.

5

Structuralist and
Post-Structuralist Approaches

> By uncovering the apparent 'logic' that informs the myth, we
> can both acknowledge the indispensable role of myth and
> myth-making for human cognition and at the same time lay
> bare the operations by which it organizes and manipulates
> reality.
>
> Froma Zeitlin[1]

A striking characteristic of ancient Greek thought is the tendency to
organize the world by means of polar oppositions, that is, by sorting
phenomena into pairs of categories that are not only different from
but opposed to one another, such as hot and cold, wet and dry, active
and passive.[2] Structuralism is a modern form of myth interpretation
that focuses on these oppositions and on the ways the Greeks used
them to structure their 'thought-world'. As a reader may guess who
has persevered this far, one of the central oppositions in Greek
thought was that between female and male. So although the approach is not feminist in origin, it has proven very useful to feminist
critics seeking to understand the workings of gender ideology. To cite
a path-breaking example: in a 1978 study of Aeschylus' *Oresteia*,
Froma Zeitlin showed that the imagery of the trilogy sets up a whole
series of oppositions in which the positive poles, including youth,
light, order, reason, and (Greek) culture itself, are associated with
male control on both human and divine levels, while the negative
poles of old age, darkness, disorder, unreason, 'barbarism', and
untamed nature are associated with female power. Beginning with
the Bronze Age figure of Agamemnon, who was murdered by his wife
and avenged by his son, Aeschylus constructs a charter myth linking

the reign of Zeus with the legal system of the Athenian democracy. As David Grene once pointed out,[3] in modern terms this scheme would be comparable to beginning a trilogy in the Garden of Eden and ending it with the signing of the US Declaration of Independence. On the divine level, the process of civilization is associated with the victory of the male-led Olympians over the older but cruder and less enlightened female deities, represented by the Furies. On the human level, 'the basic issue in the trilogy is the establishment in the face of female resistance of the binding nature of patriarchal marriage where wife's subordination and patrilineal succession are reaffirmed'.[4] By staging Orestes' trial for matricide as a debate between the older and younger gods, represented by the Furies and Apollo, Aeschylus linked the divine and human levels and portrayed the victory of all the positive forces as a victory-by-association of male over female.

Of course the female forces cannot simply be eliminated; they must be reconciled to their place in the hierarchy. This is accomplished through the mediation of Athena, a female god who as virgin daughter of Zeus and patroness of heroes is 'always for the male'.[5] It is she who convinces the Furies to accept their new subordinate place in Zeus' regime. In the structuralist perspective, such mediation is a central function of myth itself, which reconciles its audiences to the contradictions that are inherent in any ideological system. While structuralism in its original form did not study the effects of ideology on the individual, a number of loosely related approaches called 'poststructuralist' have focused on these effects. The resulting body of theory has been extremely useful to feminist critics seeking to understand how women can be reconciled to a subordinate status. Some forms of poststructuralism, in turn, have contributed to a wider movement in academic criticism called cultural studies. This interdisciplinary movement, whose practitioners can be found in departments of English, comparative literature, anthropology, women's studies, and American studies among others, has only begun to be embraced by classicists. Yet I believe it is well suited to a field that combines an emphasis on literary texts with a growing concern to integrate the methods and findings of history, art history, and the social sciences.[6]

5. Structuralist and Post-Structuralist Approaches

The structuralist study of myth was pioneered by the French anthropologist Claude Lévi-Strauss, who applied it to the interpretation of South American Indian myths.[7] But Lévi-Strauss himself made a foray into classical terrain with an essay on the Oedipus myth, and his approach was adopted in the 1960s by a group of French classicists who have used it to striking effect. The approaches called 'poststructuralist' are also primarily French in origin but have fewer classicist practitioners. Poststructuralism not only comes after structuralism but includes a critique of it, so I will consider it in the second half of this chapter. Although these two approaches are distinctive enough to deserve a chapter to themselves, they incorporate some elements of earlier approaches (especially, for poststructuralism, the psychological), and they have been used in turn to illuminate problems raised by these earlier approaches (especially the ritualist). So the present chapter is also a demonstration of how methods of myth interpretation have built on one another – or (to use a term of Lévi-Strauss') how interpretation is a form of *bricolage* or 'tinkering', taking pieces of older theories and putting them together in new ways. As we will see, *bricolage* is also an apt metaphor for mythmaking itself, which never starts with 'raw' materials but is forever making new stories out of older ones.

French structuralism

In the structural study of myth, Lévi-Strauss played a role comparable to that of Freud in psychoanalysis: his copious work laid the ground rules that have continued to be followed even as they are argued over. Lévi-Strauss' innovation was to treat myth – and culture as a whole – as a kind of language that could be analyzed using principles borrowed from the science of linguistics. The linguistic principles he used were those of Ferdinand de Saussure, himself a major innovator whose work has influenced scholars in many fields. Saussure analysed language as a system of *signs*, each consisting of a 'signifier' (*signifiant* in French) and a 'signified' (*signifié*). (I give the French words because many scholars use them even when writing in English.) The 'signifier' in spoken language is a sound; the 'signified', which cannot be separated from it, is the mental concept the sound evokes. One of Saussure's decisive breaks with earlier linguists was his insistence on the basically arbitrary nature of the sign: for example, there is no inherent connection between the sound [tɛn] and the mathematical concept of the number ten, as we can see from the great variety of words for this concept in other languages. The individual sign is useless by itself; it is in combination with other signs, in systematic *relation* to them, that it generates meaning. Lévi-Strauss argued that the same was true of myth: an individual element of a myth, such as a character or object (a king, the sun), does not have intrinsic meaning but only meaning in relation to other elements. Using the model of linguistics, in which the rules of syntax are used to generate understandable sentences in a language such as English or Latin, Lévi-Strauss set out to identify the 'syntax' of myth, the underlying principles or operations of the mind by which myths are generated.

Two further distinctions made by Saussure are essential to an understanding of structuralism. The first is the distinction between 'language' (*langue* in French) and 'speech' (*parole*). 'Language', in this specialized usage, is the system of relations between linguistic signs, whereas 'speech' is an individual utterance, the act of a person using the system. If Lévi-Strauss is right that myth is itself a language in Saussure's sense, the individual myths in their historically specific forms are the resulting 'speech'. This brings us to the second important distinction, between the synchronic and the diachronic. A synchronic analysis looks at the system in a kind of freeze-frame, at one moment in its development; a diachronic analysis looks at the evolution of the system over time. Lévi-Strauss has often been criticized for ignoring the diachronic dimension, but as Hans Penner has shown, he did not deny its importance.[8] In emphasizing the synchronic he was reacting against an emphasis on the diachronic in a number of older theories, especially theories in sociology and anthropology that insisted every culture had to progress through a series of identical stages. By contrast, Lévi-Strauss insisted that the cultures formerly called 'primitive' were engaged in the same kinds of logical operations as the more technologically sophisticated cultures.

130

5. Structuralist and Post-Structuralist Approaches

In the essay best known to classicists, 'The Structural Study of Myth', Lévi-Strauss outlines a technique of myth interpretation that involves breaking the story down into what he calls its 'gross constituent units' or 'mythemes' (on the analogy of phonemes in linguistics – the smallest units into which speech can be analysed). Each mytheme takes the form of a relation and can be expressed as a sentence; for example, 'Oedipus kills his father, Laios'. A story is obviously diachronic: it unfolds in time. But Lévi-Strauss argues that it can also be analysed synchronically, since the mythemes can be sorted into 'bundles' according to the type of relation they represent. The technique suggested by Lévi-Strauss, which reveals its origin in an era before computers, involves writing each mytheme on an index card. The cards are then organized in two dimensions simultaneously: horizontally according to the order of the story, and vertically into columns representing the 'bundles' of related mythemes. In the myth of Oedipus, for example, Lévi-Strauss found four such bundles:

Cadmos seeks his sister Europa, ravished by Zeus			
		Cadmos kills the dragon	
	The Spartoi kill one another		
			Labdacos (Laios' father) = *lame* (?)
	Oedipus kills his father, Laios		Laios (Oedipus' father) = *left-sided* (?)
		Oedipus kills the Sphinx	Oedipus = *swollen foot* (?)
Oedipus marries his mother, Jocasta			
	Eteocles kills his brother, Polynices		
Antigone buries her brother, Polynices, despite prohibition			

131

In Lévi-Strauss' reading, the first two columns consist of acts that 'overrate' and 'underrate' blood relations, respectively; the second two columns, less obviously, reflect contrasting attitudes (hostility and acceptance) toward the notion that humans are autochthonous, that is, born from the earth. In killing earth-born monsters, Cadmus and Oedipus are asserting their independence of the earth; the names that suggest trouble with walking, by contrast, reflect a belief (not attested among the Greeks, but found in several other cultures) that earth-born humans cannot walk properly when they first emerge from the ground.

In order to include the numerous versions of a given myth in the analysis, Lévi-Strauss suggested repeating this procedure for each version and arranging the versions one behind the other on a series of vertical boards. He was confident that the bundles of relations would remain consistent from one version to another – so confident, in fact, that he claimed Freud's reading of the Oedipus myth should still be considered a version of the myth itself! Most controversially, he also claimed that the structure of every myth could ultimately be expressed by the same mathematical formula, an analogy between four bundles of relations (functions) in which 'a relation of equivalence exists between two situations defined respectively by an inversion of *terms* and *relations*'. In the myth of Oedipus, 'the overrating of blood relations is to the underrating of blood relations as the attempt to escape autochthony is to the impossibility to succeed in it'.

Although it may not seem that gender has anything to do with this analysis, it is present in a latent form. As Lévi-Strauss explains,

> the myth has to do with the inability, for a culture which holds the belief that mankind is autochthonous ... , to find a satisfactory transition between this theory and the knowledge that human beings are actually born from the union of man and woman. (56)

Lévi-Strauss frames the issue as though it were a purely abstract logical problem; and surely he is right that logic is an important component of the thought processes reflected in myth. What he failed (or refused) to investigate was the political component – the political *stakes* implicit in some of the oppositions he uncovered. Claims of autochthony on the mythic plane, as Nicole Loraux has shown in detail,[9] could be used to deny the reality of women's contribution to reproduction; this made it easier to refuse them the status of citizens.

Lévi-Strauss was not a classicist, and his reading of the Oedipus myth was a one-time exercise. But his method of myth interpretation was taken up and refined by a group of francophone classicists whose best-known members include Loraux as well as Jean-Pierre Vernant, Marcel Detienne, and Pierre Vidal-Naquet. Some American classicists, such as William Blake Tyrrell, have adopted the methods of French structuralism without much change; others, such as Froma Zeitlin and Page duBois, have adapted elements of it. While these classical scholars, French and American, have borrowed from Lévi-Strauss a preference for synchronic interpretations, they have also insisted on locating their interpretations in history. To make sense of an object or a narrative element in myth, they argue, we must relate it to the social and historical circumstances in which the myth was told. Thus they focus on specific versions of myths that can be situated historically: for example, the myth of Prometheus and Pandora as told by Hesiod, or the myth of the Amazons as portrayed by the artists who decorated the Parthenon.

Vernant's essay on 'The Myth of Prometheus in Hesiod' is one of the clearest, and deservedly one of the most influential, structuralist readings of a Greek myth.[10] His analysis resembles that of Lévi-Strauss in treating several versions of the myth as complementary. Yet although he analyzes Hesiod's two versions of the Prometheus story (in the *Theogony* and the *Works and Days*) as a single myth, he justifies this proceeding not by claiming that all versions are equivalent but by arguing that these two in particular – which are contemporary and attributed to the same author – complete each other. Instead of ignoring the narrative sequence, as Lévi-Strauss did, he analyses the myth on two levels – the narrative and the 'semantic' – which are mutually reinforcing but not identical. Thus the structure he identifies is first of all a *narrative* structure, a series of events, whose order is not reversible and whose effects cannot be undone. But there is a second kind of structure implicit in the story, which is portrayed as the outcome of the narrative sequence. This is the structure of the world, and more precisely the human condition, conceived as an interlocking set of social institutions: animal sacrifice, marriage, and technology (especially cooking, symbolized by 'Promethean' fire, and agriculture). Although the myth speaks in universalizing terms, Vernant never loses sight of the fact that it is really describing the distinctive forms that these institutions took in archaic Greece.

The core of the myth, as identified by Vernant, consists of 'reciprocal offers of deceptive gifts that may be either accepted or refused' (185). At the first sacrifice, Prometheus offers Zeus a choice between two portions of the animal: the edible meat concealed in the unappetizing stomach, and the bare bones concealed in a rich-looking layer of fat. The fact that Zeus chooses the second of these portions establishes a precedent for humans to eat the meat of sacrifices while burning the inedible bones and fat as an offering to the gods. But Zeus is unhappy with the deception and 'conceals' fire from men (there are still no women) in retaliation. When Prometheus steals the 'seeds' of fire, hiding them in a hollow stalk, Zeus retaliates once again by creating a final deceptive gift: Pandora, the first woman.[11] Although she has a strong and even irresistible visual appeal for Epimetheus, the brother of Prometheus, to whom she is sent – and who has been warned by Prometheus never to accept a gift from Zeus – her beauty hides a 'bitchlike' and 'thieving' nature. What is more, she brings with her a jar of evils, including diseases, old age, and death, which she releases into the world. (It should be noted that in Hesiod's version, the woman is never told *not* to open the jar; modern retellings in which her curiosity is the source of all the trouble are patterned on the Genesis story in which Eve is told not to eat the fruit of the tree of knowledge.) The moral drawn by Hesiod is that although Zeus has successfully 'hidden' the means of human livelihood, it is not possible to hide from, or 'elude', the mind of Zeus. The human condition is such that good and harmful things are inextricably mixed: either good things are hidden and obtainable only by putting up with evils, such as hard work; or harmful things are hidden behind an attractive façade. Fire and plant foods, which

134

were originally freely given by the gods, now have to be carefully preserved and reproduced; men themselves have to reproduce by planting their 'seed' in the 'bellies' of women. The Greeks did not confuse the uterus with the stomach, but the proximity of these organs and the increased nutritional needs of pregnant and lactating women made it possible for Hesiod to suggest a symbolic equivalence, not only between the two organs but between the 'belly' and the entire woman.

Vernant's 'semantic' analysis focuses on Hesiod's use of specific Greek words, but it is comprehensible to those who do not know Greek. In fact, it could also be described as a symbolic analysis because it lays bare a system of symbolic equivalences left implicit in Hesiod's text. Thus Pandora corresponds symbolically to each of the following:

1. both portions of the first sacrifice, the inedible one because she is deceptively attractive and the edible one because she is herself a 'belly';
2. the Promethean fire, which must be fed and which 'burns' men with desire and worry;
3. the livelihood (Greek *bios*) which men must earn by ploughing the earth in which they plant seed, just as they get heirs by planting 'seed' in their wives.

Vernant concludes his analysis with another bow to Lévi-Strauss by showing how the institutions of sacrifice, marriage, and agriculture situate 'mankind' midway between beasts and gods. In a later volume co-edited with Marcel Detienne, *The Cuisine of Sacrifice among the Greeks*, Vernant worked out a more detailed version of this analysis:

Like animals, men must kill, eat, and procreate in order to survive. But in these three activities rigorous prohibitions circumscribe the domain of what is possible for humans, actions that must be both licit and pious with respect to the gods. One cannot kill just any living creature, eat just any kind of food, or couple with whomever one pleases ... Carried out

according to ritual, these activities are not only under the
patronage and warranty of the gods, they constitute religious
procedures by which men and gods are joined .. [Yet paradoxi-
cally] the union with the gods also constitutes the distance, ...
and renunciation of that state of quasi-divine felicity humanity
once knew.[12]

Pandora can be seen as a perfect symbol of the human condition
because she combines aspects of all three statuses:

> Through the charm of her outward appearance, in which she
> resembles the immortal goddesses, Pandora reflects the bril-
> liance of the divine. Through the bitchiness of her inner spirit
> and temperament she sinks as low as the bestial. Through the
> marriage that she represents, and through the articulated
> word and the strength that Zeus commands her to be endowed
> with, she is truly human.[13]

It is all the more remarkable, then, that Hesiod does not call her the
mother of all subsequent humans but only of the *genos gunaikôn*,
the 'race of women'.

It should be clear from this summary that the male-female
opposition is not an element Vernant has himself imposed but a
basic constitutive element of Hesiod's own account and, by implication, of a worldview shared by at least some of his audience. In fact,
although Vernant's analysis is that of a modern man and an out-
sider, it scrupulously avoids passing judgment or even imagining an
alternative standpoint within the archaic Greek world. It was left to
feminist scholars to extend the analysis by making explicit the
logical contradictions within the structure, which become visible
only when we admit that the male standpoint is partial (in both
senses: limited and biased). As Marylin Arthur [Katz] has pointed
out, the figure of Pandora as 'belly' is used by Hesiod to '[embody]
the principle of corporeality [and] the fact of mortality'; onto her are
'[displaced] ... all the ambiguities which mark the human condition'.[14] A Greek male could comfort himself with the fiction that his
wife's 'belly', and not his own, was the one he had to work to fill; in

the same fictional perspective, the woman's own work remained invisible to him. The supreme irony, from a feminist standpoint, is that the figure in this story who symbolizes the human condition is denied full humanity. She is the mother, not of 'all the living' like the biblical Eve, but of the 'destructive race of women'.

Like Pandora, the mythic figure of the Amazon fits the structuralist approach hand and glove. Although Amazon myths may have originated in Greek contacts with actual societies in which women rode horseback and wielded weapons, the versions that have survived are fully mythic in their neat reversals of Greek (especially Athenian) norms.[15] The male/female opposition, in structuralist terms, included polarities in roles and expected behaviour. Thus the male was associated with outdoor activities, travel, and aggression while the female was assigned to indoor activities, immobility, and passivity.[16] The primary male roles were those of citizen and warrior; of the female, those of wife and mother. Male control of women was justified as the safeguard of patriliny, the reckoning of descent and inheritance from father to son. Sons, who represented the continuity of the family, were valued above daughters, who were given away in marriage to produce sons for other families. The Amazons were said to reverse every one of these expectations: they valued daughters above sons, to the point of killing or giving away male babies born to them (as unwanted daughters might be exposed in Greek society); they assumed all the roles reserved for males in Greece, administering their own affairs and engaging in warfare. Above all they rejected marriage outright, seeking sexual contact with men only sporadically and for their own purposes – that is, for their own pleasure or to reproduce their society of women, as the Athenians claimed to need women only for *their* pleasure or to reproduce their society of men.[17] As might be expected, the Greeks consistently portrayed Amazons as losing their battles with Greek heroes, who represented the 'proper' patriarchal order.

Systematic reversals like these are not confined to myth but can be observed in ritual as well. In particular, the reversal of gender roles can be seen in initiation rituals, which often require young people to dress or act temporarily like members of the opposite gender before assuming their full adult status. The 'little bears' of

Artemis, as I noted in Chapter 3, may have acted out the wildness and aggression they would be expected to sublimate as adult women. In a complementary boys' ritual, the Oschophoria, two boys leading a procession were required to dress as girls. William Blake Tyrrell has linked these reversals to those that are so prominent in myths about the Amazons. But if the temporary reversals of ritual are considered appropriate and even required, a permanent reversal like that imagined in myth is seen as destructive. In Tyrrell's words, 'the Amazon myth concerns the specter of daughters who refuse their destiny and fail to make the accepted transition through marriage to wife and motherhood. Amazons are daughters in limbo' (Tyrrell, p. 65).

At the same time, they are also *sons* in limbo, behaving like boys stuck in a transitional phase between childhood and adulthood (like Hippolytos, whose mother was an Amazon). For this part of his argument Tyrrell builds on an earlier structuralist study by Pierre Vidal-Naquet of the *ephebeia*, the state-sponsored training of young men (ephebes) as soldiers.[18] Once again the Athenian model is used simply because we have more information about it. At the age of 18, all Athenian boys were separated from their families for two years of military service and training. During this time they were stationed on the frontiers of Attica, marginalized in space as they were in status, and engaging in skirmishes with light weapons, in contrast to the pitched fighting in which they would take part as adults. The usual battle formation in classical Greece was the hoplite phalanx, composed of tight rows of soldiers each of whom protected his neighbour with the shield held in his left hand as he fought with the thrusting-spear or sword in his right. Hoplites fought pitched battles in the daylight; the ephebes skirmished by night using surprise and trickery to compensate for their inferior weaponry. The Amazon is also said to fight in this way; as Tyrrell puts it, she is 'like the boy who, sent out to the frontier to hunt and defend the borders, never returns for marriage and a place in the hoplite formation' (76).

No wonder, then, that Amazons had to be defeated in Greek myth: if their refusal of marriage implicated both sexes, it was a double threat to the reproduction of the society and its gender system. Victories over individual Amazons or Amazon armies were attrib-

138

uted to major heroes like Achilles, Herakles, and Theseus. The Amazons were even said to have invaded Attica, either to reclaim their queen, who had been abducted by Theseus, or out of sheer desire for conquest. This group suffered the greatest defeat of all: it was said that none of them escaped alive. The Amazons' defeat in Attica became a *topos* – a conventional motif – of Athenian public speeches, parallel to the defeat of the Persians. As the orator Lysias put it, 'when they encountered brave men, they displayed spirits to match their [female] bodies'.[19]

Oratory was not the only medium in which the Greeks celebrated their victories over the Amazons. At Athens and Delphi, these myths provided the inspiration for large paintings and works of sculpture, commissioned for public buildings and paid for with public funds. Although the paintings have long since perished, they were described by the traveller Pausanias in the second century CE, and contemporary vase paintings have survived to give us a clearer idea of their iconography. In particular, it is known that 'Amazonomachies' (battles of Greeks and Amazons) were prominently displayed in two places on the Parthenon and in the Stoa Poikile or 'Painted Stoa' in the agora. In these locations they were juxtaposed with images of battles in which Greeks overcame other enemies. On each of the Parthenon's four sides, a row of metopes (square relief sculptures) depicted scenes from a different battle: Athenians against Amazons on the west, Greeks against Trojans on the north, Lapiths (a Greek tribe) against Centaurs on the south, and on the east, above the entrance, the Olympian gods against the Giants. The Amazon battle was repeated for good measure on the shield of the towering Athena statue. In the Stoa Poikile an Amazonomachy was juxtaposed with a painting of the Greek victory over the Persians at Marathon. Page duBois, followed by Tyrrell and others, has shown how this iconography creates an analogy among the polar oppositions between male and female, human and animal (the bestial Centaurs), Greek and 'barbarian' (Trojan or Persian). By organizing the polarities in this way, duBois argues, the Athenians identified the Greek male human as the norm and placed him in a central position from which women, animals and 'barbarians' were excluded by definition. These excluded groups constituted the 'others' whose marginal status guaranteed the privilege of the Greek male.

Poststructuralism

Although feminists like duBois, Tyrrell and Zeitlin have used structuralist methods in their interpretations of myth, there are some assumptions inherent in Lévi-Strauss' own brand of structuralism that make it incompatible with a feminist perspective. In particular, Lévi-Strauss makes no room in his conceptualization of culture for different standpoints or political interests; as he sees it, the source of conflict in myth is logical contradiction, not competition among social groups. On the whole, Lévi-Strauss was interested in *how* myths mean, not in *what* they mean. If myth is a language, he was interested in *langue*, not *parole*; in the rules of grammar, not the meaning of specific utterances.

Yet even Lévi-Strauss recognized that this language had an unconscious dimension: when people retell a myth, they are not conscious of the underlying (logical) contradictions it is designed to mitigate. In fact, this is the 'point' of myth in a structuralist perspective: to 'mediate', or help us live with, contradictions. The practitioners of '*post*structuralist' theory have picked up this insight and developed it in a very different way. For them, the contradictions myth is designed to mediate are deeply social and involve the unequal distribution of power and resources among groups in a hierarchy. At the same time, poststructuralists insist that meaning is never fixed or monolithic. This fluidity in the meaning of words and stories makes it possible for marginal or oppressed groups to contest the dominant patterns in a given culture.

The emphasis on social inequality in poststructuralist theory and cultural studies was contributed by Marxist scholars, especially Antonio Gramsci and Louis Althusser. The emphasis on the unconscious was borrowed from Freud, but modified in significant ways. This blend of different strands of theory has intimidated many people, partly because it is often presented in very difficult language. Because I believe it can be a powerful tool for myth analysis, I will try to explain it here in an accessible way.[21] In an overview like this, some simplification is inevitable because of the sheer number of practitioners of the theory, each of whom has shaped it in a somewhat different way. Until now it has been used by relatively few classicists, but as some specific examples will show, it can be applied to classical as well as to modern literature and culture. Some feminists have rejected it on the grounds that it emerged from a male-dominated academic hierarchy rather than from women's experiences. But other feminists have used it to uncover the processes by which women are reconciled to subordinate status – and by which they also resist that status.

The biggest sticking point for most classicists who have studied poststructuralist theory is probably its account of subjectivity. The traditional Western understanding of 'the subject', often called the 'self', is of a 'knowing, unified, rational' center of consciousness. Like Freud, poststructuralists insist that this is a fiction – that in fact the self is full of contradictions and repressed or unconscious elements. Some poststructuralists, notably Jacques Lacan and his followers, are also Freudians, who have accepted and built on Freud's basic description of the way personality is shaped in childhood. They diverge from Freud in emphasizing the role of language in the formation or 'construction' of subjectivity. The self, for all poststructuralists, is an effect of language: by entering into discourse, by saying 'I', we enter the symbolic order, which offers us a range of 'subject positions'.

> As in Saussurean theory, the symbolic order is made up of signifiers, but with an important difference. Signifiers are not linked to fixed signifieds or concepts. Language is a constant stream of signifiers which achieve temporary meaning for a speaking subject retrospectively through their difference from one another.[22]

Whereas all poststructuralists would agree that there is no ultimate guarantee of meaning, either in the conscious self or in a necessary correlation between language and reality, they differ among themselves in the amount of freedom they attribute to the subject. For 'deconstructionists' like Jacques Derrida, the play of meaning is endless and indefinitely 'deferred'; for Marxists like Louis Althusser and feminists like Chris Weedon, social structure, with its hierarchies of gender and class, is encoded and reproduced in language. Yet for both groups, the ultimately arbitrary nature of the sign can be a source of freedom. If hierarchy is not 'natural' but an effect of language, it can be resisted and even overthrown.

Most of us in the West tend to *experience* ourselves as unified subjects, so that 'common sense' makes us suspicious of alternative views. To those who consider themselves humanists, the notion of a decentered subjectivity can be especially threatening. Poststructuralists would reply that this is because the 'humanist subject' is taken for granted in most Western discourses – that of education as well as those of politics and the media. As one whose scholarly work has focused on the *Odyssey*, with its insistence that human beings can remain 'the same' for twenty years, I am myself reluctant to abandon the unified subject. In fact, I would say that for now, it is part of our shared experience of reality, however it came about. At the same time, I would urge classicists and others to try out the methods of poststructuralism 'as if' they were true, for the sake of the insights they can generate. The *Odyssey*, for example, portrays its hero as conjuring up multiple versions of himself in speech; he may be the 'same' man who left for the Trojan War, but this 'sameness' paradoxically includes a capacity for difference: the epic introduces him as *polytropos*, the man 'of many turns'.[23]

The most influential poststructuralist notion is probably that of *discourse,* as initially defined by Michel Foucault. At any given time and in any given culture, there are a number of 'discursive fields' – areas of activity, such as medicine, law, and education, in which language is used in competing ways to organize and give meaning to experience. The discourses within a given field offer 'conflicting versions of social reality, which in turn serve conflicting interests' (Weedon, 34).Within each field there is usually a *dominant* discourse that justifies the status quo and offers normative subject positions to those who use the language. Althusser described the effect of dominant ideology as a process of 'hailing' and response, as in the phrase 'she hailed a cab'. When we are 'hailed' by others, and especially by representatives of social institutions – teachers, police officers, news reporters – who seek to label us in hierarchical ways, we tend to respond by accepting the subject positions they offer. In becoming the 'subjects' of language, we can thus be *subjected* to the version of reality it offers. In Althusser's terms, we are 'recruited' by the dominant ideology; we think we are authorizing it when in fact it is 'constructing' us. The unconscious or repressed content in this system is not, or not only, a set of sexual taboos but a set of power imbalances that language helps to disguise. While basically accepting this view, Weedon insists that each of us also retains some measure of freedom to *mis*use the dominant discourse and so to resist its constraints. Because of the instability of signifiers, even traditional cultures cannot enforce a single monolithic version of reality. Thus the subject of language – the 'I' who speaks – is not *merely* subjected but preserves some agency. This agency is more limited than the freedom of choice envisioned by liberal humanism, but it still holds out the hope of change. Indeed, if language is a 'site of struggle' among competing discourses rather than a description of 'the way things are', change is inevitable.

Foucault showed that discourses are historically specific and that major 'ruptures' have occurred between the dominant discourses of different eras. This attention to historical specificity makes some forms of poststructuralism compatible with another movement in contemporary criticism called 'the new historicism'. 'New historicists', who include many classicists, put an emphasis on the historical context of literature and other cultural forms. Rather than study literary texts as independent aesthetic objects, as the 'new critics' of the mid-twentieth century had done, they look for connections between specific texts and the historical moments in which they were produced. In poststructuralist terms, they try to show how literary texts participate in the wider discourses of their times. This has revealed extremely interesting connections among apparently separate discourses such as those of medicine and tragedy, or those of political rhetoric and epic.

What does all this have to do with classical mythology? Myths, as we have seen, participate in ideology; poststructuralist theory offers a compelling account of how ideology works. Thus the theory should be applicable to the study of myths, and in fact it was used by one of

143

the earliest poststructuralists, Roland Barthes, to reveal the mythic dimensions of modern political symbols and commercial advertisements.[24] Ads, for example, offer us specific (and gender-specific) subject positions: the pencil-thin, bronzed woman drawing the eyes of all men on the beach; the construction worker rewarded with a beer for his day's work; the harassed mother thankful for the 'fast food' her husband has brought home. The ads work only to the extent that we are willing to (mis)identify ourselves with these subject positions and purchase the accessories necessary to sustain them. In the same way, myths offer subject positions to their audiences: the faithful Penelope, the dutiful Aeneas, the brave but headstrong Antigone. The traditional dimension of myth can make it seem inevitably wedded to the dominant discourse, but this is by no means the case. In particular, the fact that myths exist only in a series of different *versions* – in antiquity as in the modern world – confirms the poststructuralist insight that discourse is historically specific and constantly shifting.

The Sabine women, for example, are used in a number of Roman imperial texts to represent the subject position of wives as mediators between the males of their two families: that into which they are born and that into which they marry. Violently seized by the Romans and forced into marriage, the women beg their Sabine fathers, who come to reclaim them by violence, to accept the new status quo and merge the Sabine community with the new Roman state. Although this episode was classified as 'history' by the Romans, it belongs to that series of stories about Rome's distant past that functioned as charter myths: in all the surviving versions, the rape of the Sabine women is 'explicitly presented ... as essential to the welfare of the state, to the perpetuation of Rome's greatness'.[25] As the Sabines had reconciled their husbands and fathers, Roman women were expected to act as peacemakers between their male kin. The myth 'constructs' men and women as different not only in their relation to violence but in the basis of their need for one another; men need women to produce sons and to cement alliances with other men, but women are completely dependent on men for their livelihood. Gary Miles has shown that while all versions of the myth make the Roman 'system' dependent on gender inequality,

144

Ovid's and Livy's versions[26] are distinctive in treating this fact as problematic. Not incidentally, these versions are contemporary with the marriage legislation by which Augustus tried to reimpose traditional male controls over women which had been somewhat eroded by new forms of marriage and a high divorce rate among the elite. Miles argues that 'Ovid's narrative clearly challenges the prevailing ideology' by emphasizing the violence done to the women and suggesting that 'order at Rome is built ultimately on brute force' (188). Livy, by contrast, seeks to 'rationalize the tradition' and make it acceptable to his contemporaries by claiming that the Sabines were flattered and coaxed by their captors into accepting their lot.

There is little disagreement that elite Roman males were offered a variety of subject positions by the male-authored texts that have come down to us. The normative roles were those of soldier, political leader, and *paterfamilias* ('father of a family'), which loom large in epic, history, and oratory. But the genre of erotic elegy offered a 'counter-cultural' alternative: the poet-lover who cares more for his *puella* ('girl') than for his familial and civic duties. The defiant speakers of elegy

> do not simply conceive of their emotionally-absorbing romantic liaisons as acceptable activities; they consider them, and the poetry emanating from them, no less strenuous and praiseworthy pursuits than conventional Roman careers in business, the military and the law.[27]

The elegists imagined a new kind of relationship between men and women, one in which mutual passion was central. They even proposed an ideal of equality between lovers – at least an equality of feeling and of commitment. This was the more striking in cases where the woman was a courtesan and thus necessarily of a lower class than her elite lover (as in the poems of Propertius addressed to 'Cynthia'). In some poems the women in these relationships are even perceived by the male speakers as *more* powerful, since they are not bound by marriage and can change partners. A few of the women are also portrayed as critics, and even authors, of poetry.[28] The question thus emerges whether elegy can be seen as offering alternative *female* subject positions to match the subversive male positions it celebrates. Feminist critics have disagreed vehemently on this issue; for an especially vivid exchange of views, see volume 17.2 (1990) of the journal *Helios,* in which scholars on both sides of the question discuss with unusual frankness their intellectual and political stakes in particular answers.

The specific issue is related to a much larger one: in the poststructuralist analysis of discourse, what difference does it make whether the author of a text is male or female? Theoretically it should make no difference, since the meaning of a text is not guaranteed by the identity of its author. From a feminist perspective, however, it is important to make room for the *agency* of women, so long denied by dominant discourses of all kinds. The case of the Roman woman poet Sulpicia is especially revealing, as I will show, and suggests that feminists need to be selective and critical in their use of poststructuralist theory.

Outside the field of classics, feminist critics have increasingly turned to the writings and other cultural productions of women, which despite their participation in dominant discourses may at least be seen as expressions of female experience and agency. A female-authored text also makes the 'author-itative' subject position of writer available to women. Classicists have only a small body of work, much of it fragmentary, that can confidently be attributed to female authors (for a nearly complete survey, see Jane Snyder's *The Woman and the Lyre*). Where myth interpretation is concerned, the evidence is especially limited. This is because most surviving texts by women are lyric poems, which allude to mythic figures but seldom retell a given myth in its entirety. Yet even these brief allusions can be mined for evidence of different 'takes' on familiar mythic patterns. On the Greek side, for example, Eva Stehle has explored the ramifications of Sappho's use of myths in which young male figures are involved in erotic relationships with older, more powerful females.[29] On the Roman side, Alison Keith has shown how the poet Sulpicia uses allusions to the mythic figure of Dido to construct a new subject position for herself as a woman who is both a poet and a lover.

Before looking at Sulpicia's Dido, however, we need to consider the views of her to which Sulpicia was responding, as well as the relationship between Sulpicia's elegiac genre and the genre of epic, from which the figure of Dido first emerged. Two studies by Alison Keith demonstrate the potential of a feminist poststructuralism to uncover both the processes by which normative subjectivity is constructed and the forms that resistance to such patterns can take. In a book called *Engendering Rome: Women in Latin Epic*, Keith identifies the epic genre and its use in Roman schooling as 'technologies of gender', by means of which gendered subject positions were produced and reproduced.[30] In a related article, however, she shows how at least one Roman woman – Sulpicia – was able to recast some of these positions in revolutionary ways.[31]

Keith reveals a symbiosis between the discourse of epic and that of education. The epic texts were central to Roman (as to Greek) education at both the primary and the secondary levels. They were used beginning in 'grammar schools', not only as the primary reading matter but as a source of mythic models for emulation. In the oratorical schools for young men the epics were used again, this time as models of rhetorical strategy and as sources of epigrams – what we sometimes call 'tags of epic' – that lent the authority of epic discourse to a speaker's argument. As Keith shows in detail, the ancient commentaries on epic texts, created for use in teaching, reveal how statements about 'manly' behaviour and the place of women could be taken out of context and used to enforce a particular vision of 'Roman Order'. Keith draws special attention to the 'homosocial' dimension of schooling, 'the rituals of the ancient classroom [that] trained elite Roman youths in "male friendships, mentorship, entitlement, and rivalry" '.[32] These patterns of male bonding and rivalry would help them compete for power and influence in adult life, while elite women, who were taught at home for the most part, were excluded from this 'boys' club'. Even the practice of reciting epic passages aloud became an occasion for 'performing' manhood; Quintilian, a teacher of rhetoric in the first century CE, warned that the style of recitation should not be made 'effeminate by affected modulation' of the voice (*Institutio Oratoria* 1.8.2, trans. Keith).

One of Keith's most interesting findings is that while the epic texts themselves, notably Vergil's *Aeneid*, contain contradictions that can be read as destabilizing the norms they ostensibly endorse, the commentaries are overwhelmingly reductive. Again and again they take lines and phrases out of context to enforce both a normative 'manhood' and a normative misogyny. Servius' fourth-century commentary on the *Aeneid*, for example, notes that the phrase *dux femina facti* ('the leader of the expedition was a woman') 'should be uttered as if astonishing'; another commentator, Donatus, says the phrase is meant as an insult to Dido's brother Pygmalion, who was unable to get the better of a woman.

The mythic figure of Dido in the *Aeneid*, who rules alone as queen of Carthage until her erotic involvement with Aeneas unhinges her and leads her to suicide, was an especially important figure in the Roman construction of femininity as incompatible with political power. As described by Vergil, she would have reminded his contemporaries of Cleopatra VII of Egypt, the last independent ruler of a Hellenistic kingdom to fall before the advance of Roman imperial forces. Cleopatra's Roman lover and eventual co-ruler, Mark Antony, was seen as having succumbed to her influence, whereas Aeneas avoids a comparable subjection to Dido by cutting his ties to her at the gods' bidding. The epic includes signs that Aeneas is emotionally scarred by this sacrifice to his imperial destiny, yet the commentators – and the schoolmasters of imperial Rome, for whom they wrote – kept insisting on the stereotypes of passionate, unstable woman versus dutiful, steady man.

In '*Tandem Venit Amor*: A Roman Woman Speaks of Love', Keith turns to the work of Sulpicia, which she sees as both bridging and revising the discourses of elegy and of epic. Belonging to a social circle that included several of the male elegists, Sulpicia sought to adapt their counter-cultural stance to her own situation as an elite woman. She did so, Keith says, by weaving into her poems a network of allusions to the transgressive figure of Vergil's Dido. Like Dido, the speaker of Sulpicia's poems is concerned about *fama*, reputation, which for a woman meant largely her reputation for chastity or its reverse. Unlike Dido, however, Sulpicia '[redefines] the terms of moral judgment'.

Like the Vergilian Dido, who does not conceal her 'fault' (*culpa*) but calls it marriage (*Aen.* 4.170-2), 'Sulpicia' delights in her fault (*peccasse*, [Tib.] 3.13.9) and revels in its publication. Where Dido is the object of rumors purveyed by *Fama*, however, 'Sulpicia' publishes her transgressive passion to gain a literary reputation. (302-2)

Dido is portrayed by Vergil as the unwitting victim of Venus and her son Amor (Cupid) who, disguised as Aeneas' son, sits on Dido's lap and ignites her fatal passion. Sulpicia, by contrast, claims that Venus, won over by her poems (her 'Muses'), has brought Sulpicia's lover to her and placed *him* in her lap. In another poem (3.14), Sulpicia, summoned away from Rome on an 'untimely' winter journey by her uncle and guardian Messalla, protests the separation from her lover – and successfully resists it, to judge by the following poem, which claims that the journey has been put off. The implication is that the first poem was meant to dissuade Messalla and that it has succeeded in its aim. If Sulpicia is evoking the *Aeneid* here, it is to cast herself both as Dido, protesting Aeneas' untimely departure in mid-winter (*Aen.* 4.309), and as a rebellious Aeneas, resisting, as Aeneas does not, a command that will mean abandoning a lover. Sulpicia's use of the word *pia*, 'devoted', to describe her lover's concern for her may also evoke and invert Vergil's use of it as the epithet of Aeneas. As Keith notes, Aeneas is not called *pius* during his affair with Dido; it is only when he has decided to put his duties as a leader above his love for her that the epithet reappears (4.393). Sulpicia is not the first elegist to apply it to the devotion of lovers, but in the wake of its epic appropriation by Vergil, Sulpicia's usage acquires a polemical tone.

References to Sulpicia's poems are often prefaced by '[Tib.]' because they were preserved in a collection attributed to the male poet Tibullus that includes the work of several poets. There are still classicists who insist that the six poems referred to as '[Tib.] 3.13-18' were composed by a man (not necessarily Tibullus) using a woman's voice or persona. The issue is complicated by the fact that two additional poems in the voice of 'Sulpicia' have traditionally been attributed to just such a male author.[33] This apparently arcane

149

dispute about authorship brings back in a more acute form the question feminists have raised for poststructuralism: does it really make no difference whether the author of the 'Sulpicia' poems was a woman or a man? If Alison Keith is right, these six little poems (totalling 40 lines) recast both epic and elegiac discourse to open up a new subject position for elite Roman women: one that combines the traditionally male prerogatives of poetic ambition and of choosing a lover outside the bounds of marriage. This was an especially bold move in the era of the Augustan marriage legislation, when the new emperor was marshalling the forces of law and propaganda to curb women's sexual freedom. To ascribe the authorship of the poems to a man is to reassert the exclusion of women from the alternative subject position they propose. It is worth noting that until the rise of feminist scholarship in the 1970s, almost no attention was paid to the Sulpicia poems; if they were mentioned, it was to dismiss them as 'amateurish'. Now that they have been rediscovered and are more highly valued, it seems necessary to some scholars to deny their female authorship. Clearly, feminism has opened up new subject positions for *contemporary* women, from which they can look back to recover the possibilities for resistance to the dominant discourses of earlier eras. The fact that it is still necessary to argue for the mere possibility of female authorship in the past suggests that feminism is still by no means a dominant discourse even within the academy, as is sometimes claimed.

Dido is an interesting figure for exploring the connection between myth and gendered subject positions. As portrayed in the *Aeneid*, she evokes specific female figures in earlier literary versions of myths: most notably, Nausicaa as drawn in the *Odyssey* and Medea as drawn by Apollonius of Rhodes in the *Argonautica*, a Greek epic of the third century BCE. Both of these figures are very young, virginal women who express erotic interest (however muted in Nausicaa's case) in foreign men before their fathers have had a chance to decide on the suitability of the matches. Medea ultimately defies her father to help Jason and to run away with him. The *Argonautica* ends with Jason's triumphant return to Greece, but in its portrayal of Medea it hints at the later stages of the myth as dramatized in Euripides' *Medea* (fifth century BCE): Jason's abandonment of Medea and her violent revenge, including the murder of Jason's new bride and her own two sons.

The Dido that Sulpicia was re-writing was thus a figure already made up of literary echoes and traces of older myths in addition to the implicit parallels to Cleopatra I noted earlier. In contrast to Medea, Vergil's Dido neither elopes with Aeneas nor seeks to harm him; she kills herself instead. The threat she poses to the destiny of Rome is thus averted – at least within the scope of the epic: her dying curse is presented as the source of hostility between Rome and Carthage, which led to the Punic Wars, the most serious challenge to Roman imperial expansion. Of course, Carthage had already been defeated when Vergil was writing. Cleopatra too had been defeated and had committed suicide. In the discourse of epic, the threat of autonomous female power, both political and erotic, must be contained. But the figure of Dido could be appropriated by Sulpicia and made to serve other purposes. Even Vergil, as Barbara McManus and others have argued, occasionally portrayed both Dido and Aeneas as 'transgendered', i.e., as taking on roles traditionally assigned to the opposite gender without being castigated for it and without losing other signs of their primary gender identities.[34]

Myths are made, as Lévi-Strauss observed, of pieces of other myths. Each version is provisional, put together in a specific place and time. Poststructuralist theory can help us to understand not only how each of these versions participated in the discourses of its own time, but how it has been appropriated, re-read, and re-written by the people of later times. By this I mean not only the adaptations, such as those of Purcell and Berlioz, but the *Aeneid* itself as read by the people of different eras, and by different people within the same era. Sulpicia's *Aeneid* was not Ovid's *Aeneid*, just as Keith's *Aeneid* is not McManus' (or Ralph Johnson's or Shelley Haley's or Susan Ford Wiltshire's …). And this is not a 'problem' but a good thing.

6

Myth, Folklore, and Popular Culture

Folk and fairy tales have always spread word through their fantastic images about the feasibility of utopian alternatives, and this is exactly why the dominant social classes have been vexed by them ... So it is not by chance that the culture industry has sought to tame, regulate and instrumentalize the fantastic projections of these tales.

Jack Zipes[1]

Three tales

I

One of Zeus' many mortal lovers was Semele, the daughter of Kadmos, king of Thebes. Some say Zeus visited her in human form, but Nonnus claims he came now as a bull, now as a lion, now as a serpent. When she was pregnant with the god Dionysos, the jealous Hera came to her disguised as an old woman and asked whether she could be sure of her lover's identity. At Hera's urging, Semele got Zeus to promise her a favour, then asked him to appear to her in his true divine shape. Though he tried to dissuade her, he could not break his promise, and the hapless Semele was consumed by lightning. Her sisters spread the false rumour that she had been punished for claiming intimacy with Zeus. The unborn Dionysos was rescued and carried to term by Zeus himself, who sewed the baby up in his thigh. Much later, the full-grown Dionysos cleared his mother's name – and according to Apollodorus, brought her up from Hades to dwell on Olympus.

II

Once there was a supremely beautiful girl named Psyche who, though mortal, was worshipped as a goddess for her beauty. Venus, the goddess of desire, was overcome with anger at this, and sent her son Cupid to punish the girl by making her fall in love with the least worthy of men. Meanwhile Apollo's oracle commanded her parents to dress her in funeral garments and leave her on a steep cliff, where a monster would come to make her his bride. When they did so, a gentle wind carried her to the foot of the cliff, where she was made welcome in a rich palace and waited on by invisible servants. She was visited at night by an equally invisible but loving husband, whose only demand of her was that she never seek to learn his identity. When her sisters came in search of her and learned of her good fortune, they were overcome with jealousy and persuaded Psyche that the unseen husband was in fact the monster of the oracle, who was only waiting for her to give birth before devouring her and her child. Preparing to kill this monster in his sleep, Psyche saw by the light of a lamp that her husband was in fact Cupid, 'the kindest and sweetest of all wild beasts'.[2] But he was awakened by a drop of burning oil from the lamp, and immediately left her. Psyche then had to perform a series of four impossible tasks for Venus before Jupiter intervened to permit her reunion with Cupid – and her deification.

III

Once upon a time there was a merchant with three daughters who suddenly lost all his fortune and had to retire to a small house in the county. Two of the daughters were too proud to work, but the youngest, called Beauty, kept house for the whole family. When the merchant went on a journey to try to retrieve some of his fortune, the older daughters asked him to bring them new gowns and other finery, while Beauty, when pressed, asked only for a rose. But the merchant was unsuccessful in his business dealings, and on his way home became lost in a dense wood. He sought shelter and came upon a grand palace that was lit up but to all appearances deserted.

Finding a place set for one in the hall, he waited a long time for the owner to return but finally gave in to his hunger and then slept in a bedroom of the still-deserted house. The next morning he set out for home, pausing only to pick a branch of roses that grew in the garden. But as he did so, a frightful Beast appeared who threatened to kill him for stealing the roses. Hearing he had daughters, the Beast offered to take one of them in exchange for the merchant's life. Against her father's wishes Beauty insisted on offering herself. The Beast, instead of devouring her, treated her kindly, visiting her only at suppertime each night. Though charmed by his perfect manners, she could not bring herself to accept his repeated offers of marriage. He gave her permission to visit her family on condition that she would return to him in a week, but her sisters, who were unhappily married to men who treated them badly, detained her out of jealousy. At last she had a dream that Beast was dying and returned full of anxiety for him. When she promised to marry him, he assumed the shape of a handsome prince and explained that in her goodness she had undone the fairy's spell that made a beast of him.

Classical myth and folklore

Those who study classical myths and those who study folklore have had little to do with one another. Yet these fields have a common subject matter: traditional narratives, many of them ancient, whose original and primary mode of transmission was oral. Intuitively, we would expect some connection between the fields and their modes of interpretation. I would like to consider the reasons for their estrangement and to recommend a closer connection in the future. Cultural studies, discussed in the last chapter, provides one model for bridging this disciplinary divide and revealing the social dimensions of narrative. Increasingly, the study of popular culture has been incorporated into *courses* on ancient mythology and literature; there is no reason why it could not similarly enrich our research. In an article on 'Teaching Greek Myth and Confronting Contemporary Myths', Peter Rose argues eloquently for the pedagogical benefits of analysing recent films using the same theoretical approaches we apply to myths. Rather than collapsing the differences between the

154

ancient and modern worlds, such comparisons can help students
(and teachers) to see the value of what is radically 'other':

> A serious encounter with a *different* civilization can be liberat-
> ing [if that other civilization is presented not merely] as a
> repository of better choices but rather as a model of a social
> totality in which the consequences of choices in various spheres
> – economic, political, social, educational, cultural – introduce
> students to the very fact of social choice and thus break the
> chain of 'natural' necessity.[3]

The rift between classics and folklore studies is a rift between
academic disciplines with vastly different histories and scales of
values. The study of 'classics' can be traced back to ancient times,
while the systematic collection and study of folklore did not begin
until the seventeenth century. (As I will discuss below, women
played important roles in this process.) The term 'classic' has always
suggested 'upper class', while 'the folk' were by definition lower in
the social scale. For many generations of classicists the productions
of 'the folk' were beneath notice, while to folklorists classical myths
seemed equally irrelevant since they survived only in polished
literary forms. Classicists studied 'high culture', while folklorists
studied 'popular culture'. In the modern academy, folklore has become a subfield of anthropology. As we have seen, classics is indebted to anthropology in many ways, but the primary focus in
classics has always been literary: the analysis of texts. Since the
1970s, literary critics in English and comparative literature have
recognized that all kinds of cultural forms can be treated as 'texts'
and analysed in similar ways. This has greatly expanded the scope
of literary criticism to include media and texts considered 'popular',
such as mass market fiction, film, and television. Some folklore
scholars have themselves adopted theoretical perspectives from
literary criticism, while literary scholars have turned to the analysis
of folk and fairy tales. The result is a tentative bridge between the
disciplines. The study of myth can only benefit from this kind of
collaborative study, in which classicists should participate. As the
techniques of criticism develop to embrace new forms of cultural

production, it becomes easier to see 'Cupid and Psyche' and 'Beauty and the Beast' (for example) as points on a continuum rather than as unrelated or even opposed in their aims. A further reason for classicists to move in this direction is the fact that the best-known versions of classical myths in the contemporary world are those produced for mass-market media: children's books, comic books, films, and television. Rather than simply retreating in dismay from a phenomenon like Disney's *Hercules*, we would do better to focus our critical attention on this new creature – and, if we find it lacking, look for alternatives to it on the contemporary cultural scene.

One potential obstacle to closer ties between folklore studies and classics is the term 'myth' itself, which has been defined by scholars on both sides of the divide in ways that make it incompatible with 'folktale' or 'fairytale'. It is often claimed, for example, that myths must have gods as characters and/or must be 'central' to the values of the culture that produced them, while folktales are about ordinary humans or even animals and are primarily designed to entertain. A third category, that of 'legend' or 'saga', is often used to account for quasi-historical tales of aristocratic heroes and their families. The problem with these distinctions, as Barry Powell and others have pointed out, is that stories with nearly identical plots may be told about characters of different classes,[4] while the line between cultural centrality and 'mere' entertainment may be finer than is often thought. Thus the 'wicked stepmother' may be played by a goddess – usually Hera – as well as by a mortal woman (Phaedra, Dirce, Ino), while the 'youngest son who gets the kingdom' by outsmarting an ogre may be played by no less a personage than Zeus. It is true that most classical myths have come down to us in forms produced by and for a literate elite, so that the human characters are usually of royal or noble birth, in contrast to the protagonists of modern folktales, who tend to be of lower-class origins. Yet we should not conclude from this accident of transmission that there *were* no lower-class versions of these stories. Even if we decide that class distinctions are essential to the meaning of a tale, the act of comparing versions set in different social strata can be a valuable exercise.

A more serious challenge to the comparison of myth and folktale is the contention of Jack Zipes that myth is by definition 'codified' and authoritative, representing the interests of the powerful, while folktale belongs (at least in origin) to a counter-tradition representing the interests of the lower classes.[5] This is an important distinction, especially from the perspective of cultural studies, which seeks to understand how stories participate in social struggles. As used by Zipes in the analysis of fairy tales, it has great explanatory force. But this is precisely because Zipes does not go in search of 'pure' or 'genuine' folktale, as if we could isolate such a phenomenon. Instead he examines the hazy areas where myth and folktale (by his definitions) overlap, and where they blend with the more modern genres of fairy tale, mass-market fiction, and film. At the same time, he is scrupulous about investigating the historical specificity of each form and its relation to the ideological struggles of its time. Zipes' work, and the related work of Marina Warner, can provide a useful model for new forms of research in classics that would compare popular and elite texts, both ancient and modern, while respecting their historical and cultural specificity.

Women and fairy tales

A recent development within folklore studies that should make it especially appealing to feminist classicists is the increasing acknowledgment of women's importance as collectors and tellers of folktales – which should not be surprising if we consider that such tales often have female protagonists as well. 'Mother Goose' may be the product of imagination, but the 'old wives' whose tales we still recall were not. Although male collectors and retellers like Charles Perrault, Andrew Lang, and the Grimm brothers tend to figure prominently in academic accounts of folklore history, Marina Warner has shown that in fact many of the earliest collectors were women.[6] The collectors, who recorded the tales in writing and published them, were aristocratic or middle-class, but their informants tended to be their nurses and servants, lower-class women who were the heirs of an oral folk tradition. The retelling and publishing of such tales was a sphere of activity open to privileged women who were themselves denied access to the classical education their male peers took for granted. Thus in spite of the importance of class differences among women, there were also commonalities of experience based on cultural assumptions about women's abilities and roles. As Warner argues,

> Fairy tale offers a case where the very contempt for women opened an opportunity for them to exercise their wit and communicate their ideas: women's care for children, the prevailing disregard for both groups, and their presumed identity with the simple folk, the common people, handed them fairy tales as a different kind of nursery, where they might set their own seedlings and plant out their own flowers. (xxiii)

A review of the history of the word 'gossip' – which originally meant a godparent (god/sib, 'god-kin'), then a christening feast, then a 'tattler', especially a woman – leads Warner to the conclusion that even its negative associations grew from a recognition of the power of women's speech. Although women's 'domestic webs of information' (34) were unofficial and unsanctioned, they could have considerable influence, not only inside but outside the family unit. They could spread news and information in addition to stories, and reinforce or undermine the reputations of families and individuals. Like women's laments for the dead, which have recently been taken more seriously by scholars,[7] 'gossip' could have wider social implications than appear at first glance. 'Gossip includes mother-wit, and mother-wit knows a thing or two that They don't know, or rather, that They don't want to be known. Or, again, that They fear they don't know' (42). That this dynamic was at work in ancient Greece as well is suggested by Semonides' poem on women (seventh century BCE), in which he condemns the 'bitch-woman' who wants to know everything that is going on, while praising the 'bee-woman' who refrains from sitting with others 'when they are talking about sex'. Plato implicitly acknowledged another form of women's power – their influence on children – when he proposed in the *Republic* to censor 'old wives' tales' (377b-c).

Fairy tales also resemble classical myths in giving supernatural powers to women. As might be expected in a Christian context, the

Virgin Mary sometimes intervenes in answer to a heroine's prayer; but usually the magic is dispensed by fairies, mysterious but powerful figures whose name derives from the late Latin word *fata*, 'fate'. *Fata*, originally neuter plural, came to be seen as feminine singular – appropriately enough, since the 'three Fates' (Latin *Parcae*, modelled on the Greek *Moirai*) were traditionally personified as female, spinning the thread of life. Like the multiple gods of pre-Christian Europe, fairies intervene capriciously in human affairs and have their special favourites and enemies. Like the ancient goddesses, they have power over spheres allotted to women, and may even be portrayed as spinning. As ancient women turned to goddesses in worship, fairy tale heroines turn to their fairy godmothers. Of course, some supernatural females in fairy tales are malevolent: bad fairies and witches. But all are powerful. As Salman Rushdie has observed about that modern American fairy tale, *The Wizard of Oz*, they conjure up a world in which 'the power of men ... is illusory [while] the power of women is real'.[8]

Ancient and modern parallels

Some classicists might argue that we cannot study the oral folk traditions of ancient Greece and Rome because they have not survived. It is true that most *explicit* references to such traditions in classical literature are brief and disparaging, like Plato's quoted above. Yet I see two avenues of approach that have yet to be fully explored and that hold out the prospect of future revelations. One is within classics itself: the intensive study of the 'orality' of Homeric and Hesiodic poetry. The other is the comparative study of folklore at the international level, using the motif-index of Antti Aarne and Stith Thompson (*The Types of the Folktale: A Classification and Bibliography*, referred to as 'Aarne-Thompson').

One of the revolutions within classics in the twentieth century was the acceptance of the discoveries of Milman Parry and Albert Lord about the 'oral composition', or 'composition in performance', of the Homeric epics.[9] Using the living oral tradition of Yugoslavia as a parallel, Parry and Lord showed that a distinctive feature of Homeric poetry – the frequent repetition of phrases, known as 'formulas' and 'epithets' – had a no less distinctive function, that of allowing the poet to compose in the very process of performing a song. This complex technique was doubtless acquired in ancient Greece as it was in twentieth-century Bosnia or Serbia: through a long apprenticeship to an experienced bard. Although in this kind of tradition there can be much consistency between performances of the same song, there are always some differences as well. This inherent fluidity allows a bard to adapt the length and the details of a performance to a specific audience.

Because the heroes of the *Iliad* and *Odyssey* are all of noble birth, it is often assumed that only elite values are reflected in the Greek epics. This is largely true of the values explicitly voiced by the characters, and good arguments have been made for the view that these values are reinforced by narrative technique – by the way the story is framed and presented to the audience.[10] Yet the poetry of Hesiod, which uses 'Homeric' formulas and techniques, explicitly adopts the perspective of the landowning peasant class and offers sharp criticism of corruption among the elite. The bards themselves, we assume, came not from the nobility but from the lower ranks of the social scale. While they might perform for groups of nobles at feasts like those described in the *Odyssey*, they also competed at religious festivals, where their audiences would have included members of the lower classes. So it is not unreasonable to look for traces, even in an elite genre like epic, of an alternative 'folk' perspective. One of the few classicists to do so has been Peter Rose, who argues that even the *Iliad* presents a radical questioning of its tradition through the theme of the wrath of Achilles.[11] In the *Odyssey,* Rose believes, the hero's disguise as a beggar allows the poet to explore much more fully an 'underclass' view of his society. By portraying the aristocratic suitors as parasitic and the disguised king/hero as abused by them, the *Odyssey* poet appeals to the lower-class men in his audience and justifies the hero's bloody revenge as a righting of wrongs they have themselves suffered. In a similar vein, Norman O. Brown has argued that the *Homeric Hymn to Hermes* shows an admiration for the god's upward mobility that would have been more appealing to merchants and craftsmen than to aristocrats: 'In the *Hymn* the aspirations of the industrial and commercial classes are

projected into the figure of Hermes; their conflict with the aristoc-
racy is projected into the conflict between Hermes and Apollo.'[12]
Brown finds support for his reading in Plato's later condemnation,
from an aristocratic perspective, of the very idea that Hermes
practiced theft (102).

But the highly formalized oral tradition of the bards was not the
only kind of oral tradition. As in other cultures the world over, tales
were transmitted by parents and nurses to children, by travellers to
those they met, and by other ordinary people gathered for common
tasks such as harvesting or spinning. Traces of these genuine 'folktales' have been preserved in a few literary sources, such as the
collections of fables ascribed to Aesop; like Homer, Aesop was a
quasi-legendary figure, but in contrast to Homer he was identified
by ancient sources as a slave, and his medium, the fable, was often
assumed to have lower-class origins.[13] At the same time, there must
have been popular *versions* of tales that survive only in elite genres
such as epic. Thus a second source of insight into the 'folk' dimension
of Greek myths comes from their relationship to international tale-
types – plot sequences that have been found in at least two, and
sometimes many, different cultures. Pioneers in this area include
the Greek scholar Ioannes Kakridis and the American William
Hansen, who have offered convincing evidence that specific myths
must be variants of older tale-types that survive not only in the
folklore of modern Greece and Italy but in other cultural traditions
as well. To classicists, who often must work with a mere handful of
versions, some of them fragmentary, the advantage of such comparisons is the relative abundance of material: international tale-types
survive in hundreds or even thousands of versions. In a pool of this
size, it becomes easier to distinguish the narrative logic of a tale and
to decide which tales are really cognate. We may also become aware
that a tale-type includes elements that are not well represented in
our classical sample, because they were felt to be incompatible with
the epic genre or distasteful to the literate elite. For example, in
modern Greek folk songs about a husband who returns home after
many years and must give proof of his identity, the final, conclusive
proof is knowledge of a mark on the wife's body; Kakridis argues that
this kind of intimate detail would be unacceptable in the aristocratic

161

genre of epic, where the final proof is the husband's knowledge of how the marriage bed was built, while the identifying mark is 'transferred' to *his* body – Odysseus' famous scar.[14]

Can these approaches to oral tradition give us insights into the gender dimensions of myth? Like the other methodologies I have discussed in this book, oral studies have been dominated until very recently by the masculine viewpoint of the scholars who initiated them – and, in the case of the Yugoslav parallels, by the viewpoint of the bards, who in the Serbian and Bosnian traditions were all male.[15] But some recent work holds out the hope that closer attention to the gender of storytellers, listeners, and characters will reveal new dimensions of the myths, especially if attention is also paid to the social dynamics of a particular tradition. Rose, for example, points out that the perspective of Odysseus, which dominates the *Odyssey*, is in some ways that of a 'threatened male', to whom a central form of danger is engulfment or deception by females (Calypso, Scylla, and Charybdis are examples of the former; Helen, Circe, and Penelope of the latter). Rather than treating this sense of danger as natural and inevitable, Rose places it in the specific historical and social context of late eighth-century Greece, where growing social inequalities might well spawn the complementary fantasies of unlimited feasting and deprivation or engulfment. Thus the 'sexual ambivalence towards women' in the *Odyssey*, as in Hesiod, is 'subordinated to or combined with an overriding oral anxiety' (130) expressed in the alternating dangers of eating too much – Circe's potion, the cattle of the Sun – and of being eaten – Scylla and Charybdis, the Cyclopes and Laestrygonians. Odysseus' way of defending himself is by means of 'phallic display': drawing a sword on Circe, or winning back his wife by outdoing and then eliminating his male rivals with an almost magically potent weapon (his famous bow). Rose draws on Freudian analysis of mythic motifs and symbols, but insists that 'Freud can and should be historicized' (133).[16]

John Petropoulos has studied the related portrayal in Hesiod's *Works and Days* (582-8) of women as 'most lustful' and men as 'most feeble' in the summer when the thistle blooms and the cicada sings. Doing remarkable detective work in the folklore and ethnography of

162

modern Greece, Petropoulos has unearthed *women's* harvest songs that express longing for their husbands. He puts these in the context of the Greek grain harvest, which required several weeks of relentless labour in the scorching heat of June as men worked in teams, moving from one area to another and sleeping in the fields, while women stayed at home. His point is not to excuse the misogyny of Hesiod but to show how *both* men's and women's perspectives are reflected in the folk tradition when it is viewed as a whole.

Similar detective work has recently been done on the ethnography of European fairy tales. By looking more closely at the portrayals of gender and class difference in the tales, scholars like Jack Zipes have suggested important revisions to the ostensibly gender-neutral Aarne-Thompson index. For example, in a study of 'Rumpelstiltskin' and related tales, Zipes asks why, in the Aarne-Thompson classification, the title character is called a 'helper' when 'he is obviously a blackmailer and oppressor'.[17] The classification of the tale itself as type 500, 'The Name of the Helper', likewise ignores its 'key themes', which are 'control over spinning and the value of spinning' (58). Zipes compares earlier and later versions of the tale-type to show that changes in its portrayal of women's spinning reflect the historical evolution of textile production, which was increasingly mechanized and moved from the domestic sphere to the factory. From being a form of production controlled by women in 'Ricdin-Ricdon', an eighteenth century French version, it becomes in nineteenth-century retellings a commercial transaction controlled by men in which the heroine's only value, likewise seen through men's eyes, is as a wife and mother. Parallel to the women's loss of control over spinning and weaving is their loss of primacy as tellers and compilers of fairy tales, which occurred during the same period and for a related reason: the rise of commercial publishing. Why do we still associate fairy tales with 'the brothers Grimm'? Because of the commercial success of their collection of German tales, which in successive versions moved farther and farther away from its oral roots.

The kinds of issues raised by Zipes and Rose link the meanings of tales to the relationships between their tellers and their audiences. Whose is the narrating voice, they ask, and who is listening?

In the field of literary criticism, questions like these have inspired a method known as narratology, which looks closely at texts for what they can tell us about the *process* of narration. One set of questions raised by narratology refer to the selection and arrangement of events: what is included, and in what order? What is left out? Another set of questions refer to the source of narration. Who is identified as the narrator, or speaker, of a given piece of text? Are there internal narrators, that is, characters who also narrate? Does the narrator sometimes give another character's perspective on the action – in other words, is the narrator always the *focalizer*, the figure from whose point of view an event is told? Who are the 'narratees' – the figures, inside or outside the text, to whom it is addressed? Although designed for the analysis of literary texts, these questions have already proven very useful in the field of Homeric studies, that is, in the interpretation of texts whose genesis was largely oral.[18] And in fact the method of narratology owes a great deal to the field of folklore studies: the first set of questions I mentioned above, those about the selection and arrangement of events, were inspired in part by the folklorist Vladimir Propp, whose work on the *Morphology of the Folktale* identified a series of 'functions' that define the basic structure of the Russian oral fairy tale.[19] If narratology is practised as a purely formal exercise in isolation from the historical realities of gender and class systems, it may seem to have nothing to do with the study of mythology; but when informed by these realities, it shows us how the 'same' story can be narrated in completely different ways and to different ends. Surely this is relevant to the paradox of mythology – its simultaneous persistence and changeability.

The myth of Cupid and Psyche offers a rare example of a tale with 'folk' affinities that exists not only in a full ancient version (that of Apuleius) but in numerous modern variants, some drawn from folk traditions and some created for mass audiences. Graham Anderson has recently argued that it has more ancient variants as well, in the Greek and even in the Hittite tradition.[20] As a case study of the kinds of insights such a juxtaposition of variants can trigger, I will summarize recent analyses of some of them: the tale of Cupid and Psyche as told in Apuleius and several versions of the fairy tale of

'Beauty and the Beast'. The Aarne-Thompson tale type to which all of these have been compared is AT 425, 'The Monster (Animal as Bridegroom)'. 'Cupid and Psyche' is classified as AT 425A and 'Beauty and the Beast' as 425C, while 425B, 'The Girl and the Bull', recalls the Greek myth of Zeus and Europa. The core story involves the following elements: a mortal wife and a supernatural husband, usually disguised or enchanted in the form of a beast; the breaking of a taboo or command; the wife's separation from the husband, followed by her search for and reunion with him.

John Winkler, one of the first classicists to use the techniques of narratology, devoted a book-length study to Apuleius' *Metamorphoses* or *Golden Ass*, in which the tale of Cupid and Psyche appears.[21] The overall plot of the work involves the magical transformation of its hero, Lucius, into an ass, his misadventures in this form, and his eventual recovery of human form through the intervention of the goddess Isis. Partly because of its genre – the Graeco-Roman novel – and partly because of its lower-class setting, it is full of embedded folklore. Winkler called attention to the ways in which the apparent meaning of these embedded tales is reinforced or undercut by their narrative frame, that is, by who tells them and in what circumstances. The tale of Cupid and Psyche is presented as part of 'a mutual exchange of tales in which the roles of narrator and audience are held in turn by [a] young woman and [an] old woman' (50). The two women are Charite, who has been abducted by robbers on her wedding day, and the robbers' housekeeper, who is not named. Charite tells the old woman about her abduction and a nightmare she has had about its outcome; the housekeeper tries to soothe her with the tale of Psyche, whose similar tribulations had a happy ending. The women 'trade tales from opposite perspectives on life: young/old, on the threshold of marriage/on the threshold of death, wealthy/poor, high class/low class, real-life account/fairy tale' (51). The narrative situation thus seems to resemble the real-life situation recorded by A.K. Ramanujan (see above, Chapter 2), in which a particular Indian tale-type was told only by older women to young girls. The content of the story reinforces the comparison, for the protagonist in each case is a young, marriageable girl and the action revolves around her mar-

riage – as in the related fairy tale of 'Beauty and the Beast'. Winkler
makes much of the fact that the old woman is in the robbers' employ
and must have their interests at heart; she lengthens the tale, he
thinks, 'to keep the girl quiet for a good long time' (56). And in fact
she explicitly contrasts the interests of the wellborn Charite with
those of the robbers, whom she calls 'my young men' (4.25). But so
far is she from being their equal that she hangs herself when the girl
escapes, presumably in fear of what the robbers will do to her.[22] Why,
then, should we not see the tale of Psyche as a fantasy suited to both
women, who can identify with Psyche's ill-treatment and vicariously
enjoy her reward for endurance? This seems an excellent illustra-
tion of what Zipes calls the 'utopian' impulse of the folktale, its
potential for keeping hope alive in the face of crushing poverty or
social constraints.

Marina Warner's history of the related tale, 'Beauty and the
Beast', begins with versions that reflect a similar hope in despair:
'Tales of animal bridegrooms hold out the dream that, although the
heroine's father has given her into the keeping of a Beast, he will
change – into a radiant young man, a perfect lover'.[23] Ironically, the
first generation of women to compose literary versions of fairy tales
were French aristocrats in rebellion against the limited educations,
arranged marriages, and sexual double standard imposed on
women of their class. Warner has found that they tended to take
their models from literary sources, including classical ones such as
Aesop's fables – and Apuleius' tale of Psyche, which was 'well-known
in courtly circles'. Yet they chose to tell these tales – which even in
their classical forms had folk affinities – in the *persona* of the old
nurse, much as Apuleius himself had done. This was partly because
the nurse represented an indigenous and 'modern' French identity,
as opposed to the learning of the 'ancients';[24] but it must also have
been because the court ladies sensed the subversive potential of the
folk persona. I should add that they did not take up the cause of the
lower classes; like too many feminists since, they focused on their
own wrongs and failed to see those of their servants. Jack Zipes, who
reads the aristocratic versions from a class perspective, has no
patience with them; Warner is more sympathetic.

It was when middle-class writers took up the tale that 'Beauty and the Beast' lost its overtones of protest and took on the new function of resigning girls to their conjugal fate. The change is also due to a shift in the intended audience of fairy tales from adults to children. Madame Leprince de Beaumont, a 'working woman' who served as governess to upper-class girls in England, produced a version for her pupils that emphasizes Beauty's obedience, humility, and patience; these are the qualities for which she is ultimately rewarded. In this version,

> we can see foreshadowed, already, the Victorian angel of the house, whose task it is to tame and gentle male lust and animal instinct. We also see an intelligent governess preparing her charges for this wifely duty, readying them to find the male spouse a beast at first, but, beneath the rough and uncivilized exterior, a good man.[25]

Warner points out that the evolution of the tale in more recent times has been influenced by two important cultural shifts: a growing acknowledgment of women's sexual desires and a drastic change in our perception of animals. Whereas once the Beast's animal form was a curse and a stigma, in some recent versions it only increases his attractiveness.[26] A US television series titled *Beauty and the Beast* that ran from 1987 to 1990 cast Beauty (Catherine) as a New York attorney and Beast (Vincent) as a charismatic Robin Hood of the sewers, who after helping Catherine recover from an assault maintains an intense platonic relationship with her. A short story by Angela Carter, 'The Tiger's Bride', actually reverses the ending so that the bride too assumes an animal form.[27] Even in Disney's animated version (1991), 'the Beast steals the show': as Warner points out, 'the real animal which [he] most resembles is the American buffalo', which has come to represent the pristine state of wild nature before the onslaught of industrialization and pollution.

But as Jack Zipes cautions, some of these versions only add a veneer of feminism to the gist of Madame de Beaumont's tale, which is to reconcile women to their traditional 'helpmeet' role within patriarchal marriage. As I noted in Chapter 1, women's increasing choice of marital and sexual partners has not been matched by a willingness on the part of men to share equally in housework and childcare. Thus some fundamental aspects of the European gender system have remained intact from antiquity to the present. Zipes is especially good at uncovering the commercial and class interests served by the tales which the mass media purvey: the Disney empire, to cite a prime example, has acquired a near-monopoly on the packaging of fairy tales, which it uses to market not only books and videos but toys, clothing, and other products. To participate in the wish-fulfilment of the story, we are implicitly told, we need only purchase these products. The result is a thoroughgoing domestication of the utopian impulse that can be glimpsed in the older versions of the tales.

Is the centralization of media control an irreversible process? Are there no 'folk' left to promulgate their own subversive tales? Several recent developments suggest that while there may be few folk enclaves left in which a precapitalist/preindustrial world view prevails, there *are* large numbers of media 'consumers' who are not content with a purely passive role. Fans of television series, for example, began in the 1960s to produce their own stories about the characters. This 'fanfiction', originally circulated at events like Star Trek conventions, has expanded enormously thanks to the Internet, where it can be published instantly. If the producers of a series eliminate a favourite character or introduce a story line that fans don't like, they can produce alternative episodes – as happened in the case of *Beauty and the Beast*. If the series is cancelled, it can survive in fanfiction. *Xena: Warrior Princess* has inspired one of the greatest outpourings of alternative scenarios (and one of the greatest protests at the handling of its series finale). Some feature films have evoked a similar desire in fans to create new stories for established characters. As journalist Nancy Schultz puts it, ' "Star Wars" may belong to Lucasfilm Ltd., but in their own imaginations, the fans own the characters'.[28] Henry Jenkins, who teaches Comparative Media Studies at MIT, sees an ancient precedent:

Literature originates in the context of a folk practice, which is to say there are certain stories, certain larger-than-life protagonists who really become central to a culture. Think about the heroes and gods of Greek mythology. Historically, those characters belonged to all of the storytellers within that community.[29]

Of course, Luke Skywalker and Xena did not originate with 'the folk': they are copyrighted creations owned by corporations. What is more, not everyone owns a computer, so fanfiction is still a relatively elite medium for storytelling. But even the very poor now own television sets, and access to electronic media of all kinds is growing. It remains to be seen what the long-term effects of media monopolies will be. Some effects are likely to be repressive and conformist. But in a cultural studies perspective, control of media *production* cannot fully ensure control of audience response.

As the process of retelling ancient myths continues in our own time, we ourselves become the tellers and audiences of these tales – whether as author and reader of this book, as teacher and student in a mythology course, or as consumer and producer of videos and Internet sites. Classicists will continue to do their job of discovering how the ancient versions grew out of, and helped to shape, their original contexts in Greece and Rome. But interpretation is not limited to scholarly articles and books: it can also take the form of retellings, illustrations, online chats, or conversations over dinner. So the future of classical mythology and its interpretation belongs to all of us.

Notes

Preface: Classical Myths in Contemporary Culture

1. 'Bon(ne) à penser', in Marcel Detienne, *Dionysos mis à mort* (Paris: Gallimard, 1977), 136.

2. William J. Bennett, *The Book of Virtues* (1993), with its spin-offs *The Children's Book of Virtues* (1995), *The Children's Book of Heroes* (1997), etc. (New York: Simon & Schuster). The opening section of the original book, entitled 'Self-Discipline', includes – among many other items – retellings of the myths of Midas, Phaethon, and the eating of the Cattle of the Sun, as well as Aesop's fable of the fox and the crow and assorted cautionary doggerel with titles like 'Dirty Jim' and 'The Little Gentleman'; the section on 'Responsibility' includes the myth of Daedalus and Icarus, along with 'Little Orphan Annie' and 'The Charge of the Light Brigade'. In May 2001 these books were still selling briskly, to judge by their sales ranks on the Amazon.com website (http://www.amazon.com, 5/20/01).

3. Kris Waldherr, *The Book of Goddesses* (Hillsboro, Oregon: Beyond Words Publishing Co., 1997).

1. Myth and Gender Systems

1. To make this a manageable task, I will limit my survey to the western English-speaking world.

2. A full transcript of this episode can be found at the *Xena* fan website 'Whoosh!', http://www.whoosh.org/epguide/index.html, under 'HTLJ 2nd season (1995-96)' (1/27/01).

3. Edith Hamilton, *Mythology* (1942; repr. New York: New American Library, 1953), 47-54.

4. Thomas Bulfinch, *The Age of Fable, or Beauties of Mythology* (1855; repr. New York: New American Library, 1962).

5. Bernard Evslin, Dorothy Evslin, and Ned Hoopes, *The Greek Gods* (Scholastic, Inc., 1966). The title page indicates that Scholastic books are published in New York, Toronto, London, Auckland, and Sydney. This book was reissued without revision in 1995.

6. William Messner-Loebs and Sam Kieth, *Epicurus the Sage*, vol I: *Visiting Hades* (Piranha Press, 1989). Piranha Press is 'an imprint and trademark of DC Comics'. The story ignores chronology in portraying

171

Epicurus (late fourth – early third century BCE) as the contemporary of Socrates, Plato, Aristotle, and even Hesiod (who lived *c*. 700 BCE).

7. Laura Geringer, *The Pomegranate Seeds: A Classic Greek Myth* (Boston: Houghton Mifflin, 1995).

8. To judge by the numerous entries in the National Union Catalog of the Library of Congress, *Tanglewood Tales* may never have been out of print; the longest gap between editions (1938-1950) seems to have been occasioned by World War II.

9. Ovid wrote another full account of the myth of Demeter in his *Fasti*, 4.393-620. This is the source of the version in which the family Ceres visits is poor. Although it omits the metamorphoses of the characters and substitutes long descriptions of Ceres' travels, it does not differ significantly in its plot line and I have omitted it for the sake of brevity.

10. A systematic attempt to do this for the most important classical myths is Jane Cahill, *Her Kind: Stories of Women from Greek Mythology* (Peterborough, Ontario: Broadview Press, 1995).

11. See, e.g., Margaret Atwood, 'Circe/Mud Poems', in *You Are Happy* (Toronto: Oxford University Press, 1974); Carol Ann Duffy, *The World's Wife* (London: Macmillan, 1999); Marina Warner, 'Ariadne after Naxos' in *The Mermaids in the Basement: Stories* (London: Vintage, 1994); Marion Zimmer Bradley, *The Firebrand* (NY: Simon & Schuster, 1987).

12. Ann Suter, abstract for 'Beyond the Limits of Lyric: The Female Poet of the *Homeric Hymn to Demeter*', forthcoming in Ellen Greene, ed., *Women Poets in Greece and Rome: New Critical Essays* (Berkeley: University of California Press, date not set).

13. Aaron Tate, 'Report on the Institute of Ethnology and Folklore, Zagreb, Croatia', *OTNews* 2.2 (June 2001). In contrast to the Serbian and Bosnian epic traditions, which are better known to classicists and in which male singers predominate, Croatian epic was often performed by women. But women were active performers of other genres as well; see Celia Hawkesworth, *Voices in the Shadows: Women and Verbal Art in Serbia and Bosnia* (New York: Central European University Press, 2000).

14. The term 'sex/gender system' was created by Gayle Rubin; her pathbreaking article, 'The Traffic in Women', appeared in Rayna Reiter, ed., *Toward an Anthropology of Women* (New York: Monthly Review Press, 1975). For a more thorough description of the contemporary Western gender system from the perspective of a US sociologist, see Joyce McCarl Nielsen, *Sex and Gender in Society*, 2nd ed (Prospect Heights, Ill.: Waveland Press, 1990).

15. There were also major variations in gender systems *within* the Greek and Roman worlds, e.g., between the very different societies of Athens and Sparta. For a fuller overview of the Greek gender system, see Sue Blundell, *Women in Ancient Greece* (Cambridge, Mass.: Harvard University Press, 1995); for both Greek and Roman systems, see Gillian Clark, *Women in the Ancient World*, Greece & Rome New Surveys in the Classics, No. 21 (Oxford University Press, 1989). For a survey of the evidence from which these composites are drawn, see Elaine Fantham et al., *Women in the Classical World: Image and Text* (Oxford University Press, 1994).

16. See Nicole Loraux, 'What is a Goddess?', in *A History of Women in the West* vol. 1, ed. Pauline Schmitt Pantel, trans. Arthur Goldhammer (Cambridge, Mass.: Harvard University Press, 1992), 11-44.

17. For further discussion of this issue, see Helene Foley, 'Interpretive Essay', in H. Foley, ed., *The Homeric Hymn to Demeter: Translation, Commentary, and Interpretive Essays* (Princeton University Press, 1994), 147-9.

18. Ian Jenkins, 'Is There Life after Marriage? A Study of the Abduction Motif in Vase Paintings of the Athenian Wedding Ceremony', *Bulletin of the Institute of Classical Studies* 30 (1983), 137-45. See also E. Parisinou, *The Light of the Gods: The Role of Light in Archaic and Classical Greek Cult* (London: Duckworth, 2000).

19. In the *Partheneia* ('maiden songs') of Alcman, composed for choral performance in seventh-century BCE Sparta.

20. Judith Hallett, *Fathers and Daughters in Roman Society: Women and the Elite Family* (Princeton University Press, 1984).

21. Translations from Ovid's *Metamorphoses* are by Frank Justus Miller in the Loeb Classical Library edition (Cambridge, Mass.: Harvard University Press, 1916).

22. This increased to 13 Senators and 59 Representatives as a result of the November 2000 elections. My source for this information is the website of the Center for American Women and Politics at Rutgers University (http://www.rci.rutgers.edu/~cawp/Facts.html, 1/27/01).

23. Geraldine McCaughrean, 'Persephone and the Pomegranate Seeds', in *Greek Myths* (New York: Margaret K. McElderry Books, 1992) – also published in Oxford, Singapore, Sydney, and Toronto.

24. See, e.g., William Fitzgerald, *Slavery and the Roman Literary Imagination* (Cambridge University Press, 2000).

25. E.g. Helene Foley (above, n. 17).

26. Susan Stitt, 'Summary and Calls to Action', in *Gender Perspectives: Essays on Women in Museums*, ed. Jane Glaser and Artemis Zenetou (Washington, D.C.: Smithsonian Institution, 1994), 151. There are of course many male feminists of whom we can say, 'their consciousness has been raised' – but consciousness-raising in groups, as a technique of liberation, has been practised mainly by women.

27. For further discussion of this point, see Chapter 2.

28. Classicists often treat this paradox as 'logical' on the grounds that those with greater self-control can be allowed more freedom. I suggest that our acceptance of the ancient 'logic' shows that we still participate in its form of doublethink.

29. In the festivals of Dionysus, male actors take female parts; and in myth, at least, female Bacchants hunt and fight like men.

30. Cf. Anne Pippin Burnett, *Catastrophe Survived: Euripides' Plays of Mixed Reversal* (Oxford: Clarendon Press, 1971).

31. See n. 17 above.

32. The translation is that of Foley, op. cit., lines 101-2.

33. Kathie Carlson, *Life's Daughter/Death's Bride: Inner Transformations through the Goddess Demeter/Persephone* (Boston & London: Shambhala, 1997).

34. Christine Downing, *The Long Journey Home: Re-Visioning the Myth of Demeter and Persephone for Our Time* (Boston & London: Shambhala, 1994).

35. Harvard University Press, 1981.

36. In Mary DeForest, ed., *Woman's Power, Man's Game: Essays on Classical Antiquity in Honor of Joy K. King* (Wauconda, Ill.: Bolchazy-Carducci, 1993), 54-77.

37. *Arethusa* 15 (1982), 129-57.

38. While my own training in the ancient languages was rigorous, my college studies were divided between classics and French, and my graduate program – the Committee on Social Thought of the University of Chicago – was interdisciplinary and individualized, combining classics, comparative literature, and some work in the social sciences.

2. Psychological Approaches

1. Demaris S. Wehr, *Jung and Feminism: Liberating Archetypes* (Boston: Beacon Press, 1987), 52.

2. Wehr is unusual in combining a thoroughgoing critique of Jung's essentialism with a postive evaluation of other aspects of his theory.

3. In Robert A. Segal, *Theorizing about Myth* (Amherst: University of Massachusetts Press, 1999), 135-41.

4. This is not to deny the 'therapeutic' uses of Freudian theory or the 'diagnostic' strain in Jungian thought, just to acknowledge a disparity in the contemporary influence of each thinker.

5. Paul Ricoeur, *Freud and Philosophy*, trans. Denis Savage (New Haven: Yale University Press, 1970), 27, 32-5.

6. Sigmund Freud, *The Interpretation of Dreams* (1900; repr. New York: Avon, 1965), 9.

7. Dorothy Dinnerstein, *The Mermaid and the Minotaur: Sexual Arrangements and Human Malaise* (New York: HarperCollins, 1976).

8. See, e.g. (in addition to Dinnerstein), Nancy Chodorow, *The Reproduction of Mothering* (Berkeley: University of California Press, 1978) and Jean Baker Miller, *Toward a New Psychology of Women* (Boston: Beacon Press, 1976). Some pioneering texts in the feminist critique of Freud have been collected in Jean Baker Miller, ed., *Psychoanalysis and Women* (New York: Brunner-Mazel, 1973)

9. See, e.g., Bruno Bettelheim, *The Uses of Enchantment* (New York: Random House, 1977) and Alan Dundes, *Interpreting Folklore* (Bloomington: Indiana University Press, 1980); for critiques of Bettelheim see Segal (above, n. 3), ch. 5, and Jack Zipes, *Breaking the Magic Spell: Radical Theories of Folk and Fairy Tales* (Austin: University of Texas Press, 1979), ch. 6.

10. Richard Caldwell, *The Origin of the Gods: A Psychoanalytic Study of Greek Theogonic Myth* (New York: Oxford University Press, 1989), 19. Caldwell's second chapter is a good succinct presentation of the essentials of Freudian theory; my summary here is heavily indebted to it.

11. Ibid., 21.

12. See Chodorow (above, n. 8), 46-8.

13. For a historical overview of these feminist critiques, see Edith Kurzweil, *Freudians and Feminists* (Boulder, Colo. & Oxford: Westview Press, 1995).

14. Sigmund Freud, *Introductory Lectures on Psycho-Analysis*, 1916-17; repr. 1963 in *The Standard Edition of the Complete Psychological Works of Sigmund Freud*, ed. James Strachey (London: Hogarth Press), vol. 15, 178.

15. In an alternative but parallel tradition preserved, e.g., in Aeschylus' *Prometheus Bound*, Zeus had to avoid marriage with the Nereid Thetis, who was destined to bear a son stronger than his father.

16. Boston: Beacon Press, 1968; repr. Princeton University Press, 1992.

17. Alan Dundes, a folklorist who has championed psychoanalytic approaches, points out that from the perspective of his discipline, the 'hero pattern' is a widespread Indo-European folk tale type that has been subdivided into more specific types in the Aarne-Thompson *Motif-Index of Folk Literature* (6 vols., Indiana University Press, 1955-58); the story of Perseus, for example, fits type 300, 'the Dragon-Slayer'. See Dundes, 'The Hero Pattern and the Life of Jesus', in *Interpreting Folklore* (n. 9 above), and Chapter 6 below.

18. For a fascinating account of splitting and its many possible implications in myth, see Wendy Doniger, *Splitting the Difference: Gender and Myth in Ancient Greece and India* (University of Chicago Press, 1999).

19. A good recent example is the hero of the wildly popular children's book *Harry Potter and the Sorcerer's Stone* by J.K. Rowling (New York: Scholastic Inc., 1997).

20. Caldwell (n. 10 above), 64.

21. Dundes (n. 9 above), 239.

22. Caldwell, 65.

23. Freud's equation of flight with penile erection finds unexpected support in the many Greek images of 'phallus-birds' – birds with phalluses for heads – and in the portrayal of Eros, 'Desire', with wings. For an especially vivid description of desire as the experience of growing wings, see Plato, *Phaedrus*, 251a-252c.

24. Page duBois, *Sowing the Body: Psychoanalysis and Ancient Representations of Women* (University of Chicago Press, 1988).

25. Peter Rose, *Sons of the Gods, Children of Earth: Ideology and Literary Form in Ancient Greece* (Ithaca: Cornell University Press, 1992), ch. 2; for futher discussion, see Chapter 6 below.

26. Python is actually a masculine name; Slater is referring to the unnamed female dragon slain by Apollo in the *Hymn*, lines 300-4.

27. Some European folktales can be seen to share a common source with the classical myths they resemble (see ch. 6). Yet this begs the question of the *survival* of mythic patterns. As Peter Rose has argued, 'the sense of immutability of psychic phenomena to orthodox Freudians derives largely from the cultural continuity, not least in sexual ideology, between ancient Greece and our own time' (above, n. 25, 133).

28. Marilyn Arthur [Katz], 'Cultural Strategies in Hesiod's *Theogony*', *Arethusa* 15 (1982) 63-82.

175

29. The extant *Hymn* is in two distinct parts and may be a conflation of two earlier poems, the first devoted to the Apollo of Delos (often referred to as the Delian Hymn) and the second to the Apollo of Delphi (referred to as the Pythian Hymn).

30. 'The Indian Oedipus', in *Oedipus: A Folklore Casebook*, ed. Lowell Edmunds and Alan Dundes (New York: Garland Publishing, 1984), 234-61.

31. Marianne Hirsch, *The Mother-Daughter Plot: Narrative, Psychoanalysis, Feminism* (Bloomington: Indiana University Press, 1989).

32. Bettelheim made a rigid distinction between myth and fairy tale, considering only the latter therapeutic; but he was thinking specifically of the effects of fairy tales on children. His rigid separation of myth and fairy tale has been challenged by Segal (above, n. 3, ch. 5).

33. Edward F. Edinger, *Ego and Archetype: Individuation and the Religious Function of the Psyche* (New York: Putnam's Sons for the C.G. Jung Foundation, 1972), 3.

34. Ibid., 65.

35. But Bernard Sergent has argued that pederastic abduction can serve an initiatory purpose in myth and ritual; see his *Homosexuality in Greek Myth*, trans. Arthur Goldhammer (Boston: Beacon Press, 1986).

36. Compare Carol Pearson's *The Hero Within: Six Archetypes We Live By* (San Francisco: Harper & Row, 1986), which does a better job of arguing for gender-neutral archetypes. See also Wehr (n. 1 above), ch. 6.

37. Tragedy is a major exception: a genre where female protagonists are common. Yet the plots of tragedy , even when they revolve around male protagonists, do not reflect the 'hero pattern' discussed in this chapter, which is more typical of epic and folktale.

38. The original title, *Metamorphoses*, has traditionally been avoided, probably to prevent confusion with Ovid's work of the same name.

39. Other feminist Jungian readings of the myth are those of Christine Downing (*Psyche's Sisters: ReImagining the Meaning of Sisterhood* [San Francisco: Harper & Row, 1988]), Gisela Labouvie-Vief (*Psyche and Eros: Mind and Gender in the Life Course* [Cambridge University Press, 1994]), and Marie-Louise von Franz (*The Golden Ass of Apuleius: The Liberation of the Feminine in Man* [Boston: Shambhala Publications, 1992]).

40. Erich Neumann, *Amor and Psyche: The Psychic Development of the Feminine: A Commentary on the Tale by Apuleius*, trans. Ralph Manheim, 1956; repr. New York: Harper & Row, 1962. 'Amor' and 'Cupid' are the two Latin names for the Greek 'Eros', the god who is a personification of sexual desire and usually portrayed as the son of Aphrodite (Roman Venus). Neumann uses the Greek names despite the fact that Apuleius wrote in Latin.

41. Yet he is still cited with praise and even a tone of reverence in some recent works, e.g., Labouvie-Vief (n. 39 above), 15.

42. Jean Shinoda Bolen, *Goddesses in Everywoman: A New Psychology of Women* (New York: Harper & Row, 1984), 5-7.

43. See, e.g., Bernard Sergent (above, n. 35), and John Makowski, 'Nisus & Euryalus: A Platonic Relationship', *Classical Journal* 85.1 (1989), 1-15.

44. E.g., Hélène Cixous and Catherine Clément, *The Newly Born*

Woman, trans. Betsy Wing (Minneapolis: University of Minnesota Press, 1986; first French ed. 1975); Luce Irigaray, *Speculum of the Other Woman*, trans. Gillian C. Gill (Ithaca: Cornell University Press, 1985; first French ed.1974); Adrienne Rich, 'Compulsory Heterosexuality and Lesbian Experience', *Signs* 5 (1980), 631-60.

45. Cixous, *The Newly Born Woman*, 67 and 69; I have modified the last clause of the translation to reflect my understanding of the original.

46. Sappho is of course the one well-known exception to the absence from the Western canon of women's voices expressing love of other women – and all but one of her surviving texts are fragmentary.

3. Myth and Ritual

1. For contrasting views of the roles of women in Greek blood sacrifice, see Marcel Detienne, 'The Violence of Wellborn Ladies: Women in the Thesmophoria', in *The Cuisine of Sacrifice among the Greeks*, ed. Detienne and Jean-Pierre Vernant , trans. Paula Wissing (University of Chicago Press, 1989), 129-47, and Robin Osborne, 'Women and Sacrifice in Classical Greece', *Classical Quarterly* 43 (1993), 392-405.

2. A deliberately monstrous exception is Clytemnestra in Aeschylus' *Agamemnon*, whose murder of her husband is sometimes described as a (corrupted) 'sacrifice' (e.g. *thumatos*, 1117; *epithusas*, 1504).

3. Selected lectures had been open to women since 1870, and the first five residential students were admitted in 1871. There was another women's college, Girton, and beginning in 1881 women could take the University examinations, but they received 'certificates' rather than actual degrees until 1948. See Sandra Peacock, *Jane Ellen Harrison: The Mask and the Self* (New Haven: Yale University Press, 1988), 34-40. This pioneering biography of Harrison is marred by an over-emphasis on orthodox Freudian psychologizing of its subject. See now *The Invention of Jane Harrison* by Mary Beard (Cambridge, Mass.: Harvard University Press, 2000).

4. Robert Ackerman, *The Myth and Ritual School: J.G. Frazer and the Cambridge Ritualists* (New York: Garland, 1991), 67.

5. For a discussion of the attacks and their consequences for the field of classics, see Moses I. Finley, 'Anthropology and the Classics', in *The Use and Abuse of History* (NY: Viking Press, 1975), 102-19.

6. William M. Calder III, 'Jane Harrison's Failed Candidacies for the Yates Professorship (1888, 1896): What Did Her Colleagues Think of Her?', in *The Cambridge Ritualists Reconsidered*, ed. Calder (Atlanta: Scholars Press, 1991), 37-59. See Thomas W. Africa's essay in the same volume for another example of this kind of personalized assessment.

7. Ackerman (n. 4 above), 67.

8. H.S. Versnel, 'What's Sauce for the Goose is Sauce for the Gander: Myth and Ritual, Old and New', in *Approaches to Greek Myth*, ed. Lowell Edmunds (Baltimore: Johns Hopkins University Press, 1990), 23-90. Even Versnel, who is in a sense rehabilitating Harrison, feels obliged to cite other scholars' 'virtually unanimous finding' that her work lacked consistency and logic (31). As Ackerman's volume shows, inconsistency is much more characteristic of Frazer's work, which is seldom criticized for it.

9. J.E. Harrison, *Mythology and Monuments of Ancient Athens* (London: Macmillan, 1890), iii.

10. Tina Passman, 'Out of the Closet and into the Field: Matriculture, the Lesbian Perspective, and Feminist Classics', in *Feminist Theory and the Classics*, ed. Nancy Sorkin Rabinowitz and Amy Richlin (New York: Routledge, 1993), 181-208.

11. In an 'Excursus' published as part of *Themis*, Harrison's fellow-ritualist Gilbert Murray found traces of the original pattern in each of the surviving tragedies.

12. The points assembled here are found in chs 1, 2, and 5 of *Themis*.

13. Harrison notes that Euripides in the *Bacchae*, 120-5, creates a link between the Kouretes and those who dance in honour of Dionysus.

14. In addition to repeated references in footnotes to Harrison's work, he cites *Themis* in the 'Preface to the English Edition' (1983) of *Homo Necans* as a work that, before his own, 'introduced ... functionalism to the study of Greek religion' (xiii).

15. English ed. trans. Peter Bing (Berkeley: University of California Press, 1983); orig. German ed. 1972.

16. Among the works cited by Burkert are two books that helped to popularize this theory: Desmond Morris, *The Naked Ape* (1967) and Robert Ardrey, *The Hunting Hypothesis* (1976).

17. See Matt Cartmill, *A View to a Death in the Morning: Hunting and Nature through History* (Cambridge, Mass.: Harvard University Press, 1993), ch. 2.

18. A pioneering article was Sally Linton's 'Woman the Gatherer: Male Bias in Anthropology', in *Women in Cross-Cultural Perspective*, ed. Sue Ellen Jacobs (Champaign, Ill.: University of Illinois Press, 1971). Other important works include Sarah Blaffer Hrdy, *The Woman That Never Evolved* (Cambridge, Mass.: Harvard University Press, 1981), Nancy Tanner and Adrienne Zihlman, 'Women in Evolution. Part I', *Signs* 1 (1976) 585-608, and the essays in *Woman the Gatherer*, ed. Frances Dahlberg (New Haven: Yale University Press, 1981).

19. Cf. Agnes Estioko-Griffin and P. Bion Griffin, 'Woman the Hunter: The Agta', in Dahlberg, 121-51.

20. Donna Haraway, *Primate Visions: Gender, Race and Nature in the World of Modern Science* (New York: Routledge, 1989).

21. Mary Zeiss Stange, *Woman the Hunter* (Boston: Beacon Press, 1997), 50.

22. The same approaches are used in studies of male initiation; see especially Bernard Sergent, *Homosexuality in Greek Myth* (Boston: Beacon Press, 1986).

23. It would be more accurate to speak of women's cultures in the plural, since Greek and Roman ritual varied in its details from place to place and rites were sometimes segregated not only by sex but by class or marital status.

24. See Bella Zweig, 'The Primal Mind: Using Native American Models for the Study of Women in Ancient Greece', in Rabinowitz and Richlin (n. 10 above), 145-80.

25. Ken Dowden, *The Uses of Greek Mythology* (London: Routledge, 1992), 105.

26. Ken Dowden, *Death and the Maiden: Girls' Initiation Rites in Greek Mythology* (London: Routledge, 1989).

27. Helen King, 'Bound to Bleed: Artemis and Greek Women', in *Images of Women in Antiquity*, ed. Averil Cameron and Amélie Kuhrt (Detroit: Wayne State University Press, 1983, repr. 1993), 120.

28. Helene P. Foley, *Ritual Irony: Poetry and Sacrifice in Euripides* (Ithaca: Cornell University Press, 1985), 85.

29. See Ken Dowden, *The Uses of Greek Mythology* (n. 25 above), 106, and *Death and the Maiden* (n. 26), 182-92.

30. Phyllis Katz, 'Io in the *Prometheus Bound*: A Coming of Age Paradigm for the Athenian Community', in Mark W. Padilla, ed., *Rites of Passage in Ancient Greece: Literature, Religion, Society* (Lewisburg, Pa.: Bucknell University Press, 1999), 129-47.

31. Paula Perlman, 'Acting the She-Bear for Artemis', *Arethusa* 22 (1989), 111-33.

32. In fact, the bear does give birth and nurse its young during a winter period of 'dormancy' (not a true hibernation).

33. Stange (n. 21 above), chs. 4 and 5.

4. Myth as 'Charter'

1. Matthias Hermanns, *The Indo-Tibetans* (Bombay, 1954), 66 ff., quoted in Mircea Eliade, *Myth and Reality*, trans. Willard R. Trask (NY: Harper & Row, 1963), 7.

2. Bronislaw Malinowski, 'Myth in Primitive Psychology', 1926, repr. in *Malinowski and the Work of Myth*, ed. Ivan Strenski (Princeton University Press, 1992), 82.

3. But see Paul Cartledge, *The Greeks: A Portrait of Self and Others* (Oxford University Press, 1993), 24-6.

4. Mircea Eliade, *Myth and Reality* (above, n. 1), 5-6.

5. See, e.g., Phyllis Trible, *God and the Rhetoric of Sexuality* (Philadelphia: Fortress Press, 1978), and Carol Meyers, *Discovering Eve: Ancient Israelite Women in Context* (Oxford University Press, 1988).

6. See Peter Rose, 'The Case for Not Ignoring Marx in the Study of Women in Antiquity', in *Feminist Theory and the Classics*, ed. Nancy Sorkin Rabinowitz and Amy Richlin (NY: Routledge, 1993), 211-37.

7. In *Lost Goddesses of Early Greece: A Collection of Pre-Hellenic Mythology* (Berkeley, California: Moon Books, 1978), 41-2.

8. In *She Rises Like the Sun: Invocations of the Goddess by Contemporary American Women Poets*, ed. Janine Canan (Freedom, California: Crossing Press, 1989), 32-3.

9. For a good sympathetic introduction to the movement, see Cynthia Eller, *Living in the Lap of the Goddess* (New York: Crossroad, 1993). Eller's

179

later book, *The Myth of Matriarchal Prehistory* (Boston: Beacon Press, 2000) is much more critical.

10. Carol P. Christ, *Laughter of Aphrodite: Reflections on a Journey to the Goddess* (San Francisco: Harper & Row, 1988).

11. Ruth Tringham and Margaret Conkey, 'Rethinking Figurines: A Critical View from Archaeology of Gimbutas, the "Goddess" and Popular Culture', in Lucy Goodison and Christine Morris, eds., *Ancient Goddesses: The Myths and the Evidence* (Madison: University of Wisconsin Press, 1998), 22-45.

12. 'Twin Peaks: The Archaeologies of Çatalhöyük' , in Goodison and Morris, 56.

13. Marija Gimbutas, *The Goddesses and Gods of Old Europe* (Berkeley: University of California Press, 1982); *The Living Goddesses* (Berkeley: University of California Press, 1999).

14. See Kelley Hays Gilpin, 'Feminist Scholarship in Archaeology', *Annals of the American Academy of Political and Social Science* 571 (2000), 89-106.

15. Clifford Geertz, *The Interpretation of Cultures* (New York: Basic Books, 1973), 118. William Doty makes use of this distinction between 'model of' and 'model for' in *Mythography*, his survey of interpretive approaches to myth and ritual (University of Alabama Press, 1986).

16. Above, n. 11.

17. The Cambridge ritualists also subscribed to this view; see discussion in Chapter 3. For a detailed history showing that Darwin was a participant in, but not the instigator of, this trend in scholarship, see Marvin Harris, *The Rise of Anthropological Theory* (NY: Crowell, 1968), esp. p. 143.

18. Augustine (fifth century CE) says he found the story in the much earlier work of the Roman scholar Varro (first century BCE).

19. Froma Zeitlin, 'The Dynamics of Misogyny: Myth and Mythmaking in the *Oresteia*', *Arethusa* 11 (1978) 149-84, repr. in *Playing the Other: Gender and Society in Classical Greek Literature* (University of Chicago Press, 1996), 87-119. This important article will be discussed further in Chapter 5.

20. Joan Bamberger, 'The Myth of Matriarchy: Why Men Rule in Primitive Society', in Louise Lamphere and Michelle Rosaldo, eds., *Woman, Culture and Society* (Stanford University Press, 1974), 263-80.

21. C. Scott Littleton, *The New Comparative Mythology*, 3rd ed. (Berkeley: University of California Press, 1982, 3. This is an excellent introduction to the work of Dumézil, whose own writing is copious and difficult for non-specialists.

22. As Jaan Puhvel puts it, '*Quirinus* was the divine embodiment of the Romans (Quirites) at peace'; his name, derived from a proto-form **Co-Virinos*, contains the root for 'male' that survives in the English word 'virile' (from Latin *vir*). *Comparative Mythology* (Baltimore: Johns Hopkins University Press, 1987), 150. An asterisk before a form is the conventional way of indicating that it is never found in written texts but has been deduced from other attested words.

23. For a fuller account of these comparisons, see Puhvel, *Comparative Mythology*, ch. 9.

180

24. For more examples from Sanskrit and other IE languages, see Calvert Watkins, *How to Kill a Dragon: Aspects of Indo-European Poetics* (New York: Oxford University Press, 1995), 8.

25. Miriam Robbins Dexter, *Whence the Goddesses: A Source Book* (NY: Teachers College Press, 1990), 35.

26. See index entries under 'transfunctional goddess' in Puhvel's index, esp. p. 62 (the Indian Sarasvati) and 103 (the Iranian Anahita). He also sees traces of this goddess in Athena and Juno.

27. Wendy Doniger O'Flaherty, *Women, Androgynes, and Other Mythical Beasts* (University of Chicago Press, 1980); Wendy Doniger, *Splitting the Difference: Gender and Myth in Ancient Greece and India* (University of Chicago Press, 1999).

28. Watkins (above, n. 24). A warning to the nonspecialist reader: this book is studded with untranslated quotations of French and German scholarship.

29. See especially Bruce Lincoln, *Myth, Cosmos, and Society: Indo-European Themes of Creation and Destruction* (Cambridge, Mass.: Harvard University Press, 1986), ch. 1.

30. Puhvel (above, n. 22), ch. 17.

31. Lincoln (above, n. 29), 45.

32. Puhvel, 266.

33. J.P. Mallory, *In Search of the Indo-Europeans: Language, Archaeology and Myth* (London: Thames & Hudson, 1989), 266. Cf. Martin Bernal's important, if controversial, study of racist tendencies in nineteenth and twentieth century classical scholarship in *Black Athena* vol. 1 (New Brunswick, NJ: Rutgers University Press, 1987).

34. Recent research on Eliade, Dumézil, Jung, and Joseph Campbell has revealed that each flirted with reactionary politics at some time in his life. For a balanced discussion, see Robert Ellwood, *The Politics of Myth: A Study of C.G. Jung, Mircea Eliade, and Joseph Campbell* (Albany: SUNY Press, 1999).

35. Bruce Lincoln, *Discourse and the Construction of Society: Comparative Studies of Myth, Ritual, and Classification* (NY: Oxford University Press, 1989).

36. For some specific political uses of such mythic descent in ancient Greece, see J.M. Hall, *Ethnic Identity in Greek Antiquity* (Cambridge University Press, 1997), 36-38, 43.

37. Lincoln, *Discourse* (above, n. 35), 6-7.

5. Structuralist and Post-Structuralist Approaches

1. 'The Dynamics of Misogyny: Myth and Mythmaking in the *Oresteia*', *Arethusa* 11 (1978) 149-84, repr. in *Playing the Other* (University of Chicago Press, 1996), 87-119.

2. See, e.g., Paul Cartledge, *The Greeks: A Portrait of Self and Others* (Oxford University Press, 1993), 11-16 and passim. Some would argue that 'polar' thinking is a characteristic of human thought in general. Lévi-

Strauss (see below) attributed it to the Amazonian Indian cultures he studied as well as to the Greeks.

3. In a course on the *Oresteia* which I attended in the 1970s.

4. Zeitlin (above, n. 1), 159.

5. *Eumenides* 737; the translation is that of Richmond Lattimore, in *Aeschylus I: The Oresteia* (University of Chicago Press, 1953), 161.

6. A fuller argument for the value of cultural studies to classics may be found in Seth Schein, 'Cultural Studies and Classics: Contrasts and Opportunities', in Thomas Falkner, Nancy Felson, and David Konstan, eds., *Contextualizing Classics: Ideology, Performance, Dialogue* (Lanham, MD: Rowman & Littlefield, 1999), 285-99.

7. A different form of structural analysis, developed earlier in the twentieth century by the Russian Vladimir Propp, will be considered briefly in Chapter 6.

8. Hans Penner, 'Structuralism, Anthropology and Lévi-Strauss', in *Teaching Lévi-Strauss* (Atlanta: Scholars Press, 1989). This collection includes 'The Structural Study of Myth', the essay by Lévi-Strauss discussed below.

9. Nicole Loraux, *The Children of Athena*, trans. Caroline Levine (Princeton University Press, 1993), orig. French ed. 1984; *Born of the Earth: Myth and Politics in Athens*, trans. Selina Stewart (Ithaca: Cornell University Press, 2000), orig. French ed. 1996.

10. Jean-Pierre Vernant, 'The Myth of Prometheus in Hesiod', in *Myth and Society in Ancient Greece*, trans. Janet Lloyd (NY: Zone Books, 1988), 183-201; orig. French ed. 1974.

11. She is given the name Pandora only in the *Works and Days*, but I accept Vernant's view (which is also the scholarly consensus) that a Greek audience would have identified the woman in the *Theogony* as Pandora.

12. Vernant, 'At Man's Table', in Marcel Detienne and J.-P. Vernant, eds., *The Cuisine of Sacrifice among the Greeks*, trans. Paula Wissing (University of Chicago Press, 1989), 74; orig. French ed. 1979.

13. Vernant 1988 (n. 10 above), 199.

14. Marylin B. Arthur [Katz], 'The Dream of a World without Women: Politics and the Circles of Order in the *Theogony* Prooemium', *Arethusa* 16 (1983), 112.

15. For archaeological evidence of cultures in which women rode and used weapons, see Jeannine Davis-Kimball, 'Sauro-Sarmatian Women: New Gender Identities', *Journal of Indo-European Studies* 25 (1997), 327-43, and the website of the Center for the Study of Eurasian Nomads, [http://www.csen.org]; for a British example recently discovered, see *BBC History* 2.7 (July 2001), 34-5.

16. Another influential essay of Vernant's explores this polarity as reflected in the divine figures of Hestia, goddess of the hearth, and Hermes the messenger-god: 'Hestia-Hermes: The Religious Expression of Space and Movement in Ancient Greece', in *Myth and Thought among the Greeks* (London: Routledge & Kegan Paul, 1983), 127-75; orig. French ed. 1965.

17. For a much fuller analysis of these oppositions, see ch. 3 of William

Blake Tyrrell's *Amazons: A Study in Athenian Mythmaking* (Baltimore: Johns Hopkins University Press, 1984).

18. Pierre Vidal-Naquet, 'The Black Hunter and the Origin of the Athenian *Ephebia*', in *The Black Hunter: Forms of Thought and Forms of Society in the Greek World*, trans. Andrew Szegedy-Maszak (Baltimore: Johns Hopkins University Press, 1986), 106-28; orig. French ed. 1981.

19. Funeral Speech par. 5, in *Lysias*, trans. S.C. Todd (Austin: University of Texas Press, 2000), 28. In fact, the usual Greek word for bravery, *andreia*, includes the root for 'man' and implies virility – thereby 'virtually [excluding] women etymologically from the possibility of experiencing [it]' (Paul Cartledge, *The Greeks*, n. 2 above, 68-9).

20. Page duBois, *Centaurs and Amazons* (Ann Arbor: University of Michigan Press, 1982), 4-5.

21. Fuller accessible accounts of the theory may be found in Catherine Belsey, *Critical Practice* (London: Methuen, 1980) and Chris Weedon, *Feminist Practice and Poststructuralist Theory* (Oxford: Blackwell, 1987).

22. Weedon, 52

23. An eloquent plea for the usefulness of poststructuralist approaches in classics can be found in John Peradotto's *Man in the Middle Voice: Name and Narration in the Odyssey* (Princeton University Press, 1990).

24. Roland Barthes, *Mythologies*, selected and trans. by Annette Lavers (London: J. Cape, 1972).

25. Gary B. Miles, 'The First Roman Marriage and the Theft of the Sabine Women', in Ralph Hexter and Daniel Selden, eds., *Innovations of Antiquity* (New York: Routledge, 1992), 187.

26. Ovid's appears in *Fasti* 3.167-258, Livy's in Book 1 (chs. 9-13) of his history.

27. Judith P. Hallett, 'The Role of Women in Roman Elegy: Counter-Cultural Feminism', in John Peradotto and J.P. Sullivan, eds, *Women in the Ancient World* (Albany: State University of NY Press, 1984), 241-2.

28. Judith P. Hallett, 'Contextualizing the Text: The Journey to Ovid', *Helios* 17 (1990), 187-95.

29. Eva Stehle, 'Sappho's Gaze: Fantasies of a Goddess and a Young Man', *differences* 2 (1990), 88-125.

30. A.M. Keith, *Engendering Rome: Women in Latin Epic* (Cambridge University Press, 2000). The phrase 'technologies of gender' is borrowed from Teresa De Lauretis, *Technologies of Gender* (Bloomington: Indiana University Press, 1987).

31. Alison Keith, '*Tandem Venit Amor*: A Roman Woman Speaks of Love', in Judith P. Hallett and Marilyn B. Skinner, eds., *Roman Sexualities* (Princeton University Press, 1997), 295-310.

32. The term 'homosocial' and the embedded quotation are borrowed from Eve Kossofsky Sedgwick, *Between Men: English Literature and Male Homosocial Desire*, 2nd ed. (NY: Columbia University Press, 1992).

33. For a review of the issue which concludes that the two additional poems are also by Sulpicia, see Holt Parker, 'Sulpicia, the *Auctor de Sulpicia*, and the Authorship of 3.9 and 3.11 of the Corpus Tibullianum', *Helios* 21 (1994), 39-62.

34. Barbara McManus, *Classics and Feminism: Gendering the Classics* (New York: Twayne, 1997), ch. 4.

6. Myth, Folklore, and Popular Culture

1. Jack Zipes, *Breaking the Magic Spell: Radical Theories of Folk and Fairy Tales* (Austin: University of Texas Press, 1979), 3.

2. The translation is that of Ralph Manheim in Erich Neumann's *Amor and Psyche* (NY: Harper & Row, 1956), 25.

3. Peter Rose, 'Teaching Greek Myth and Confronting Contemporary Myths', in *Classics and Cinema*, ed. Martin Winkler (Lewisburg, Pa.: Bucknell University Press, 1991), 19.

4. Powell's textbook, *Classical Myth* (Upper Saddle River, NJ: Prentice-Hall, Inc., 3rd ed. 2001), points out the folktale patterns in Greek and Roman tales usually classified as 'divine myth' or 'legend'. Cora Sowa, *Traditional Themes and the Homeric Hymns* (Chicago: Bolchazy-Carducci, 1984), argues that 'all of the themes can have either human or divine protagonists' (30).

5. Jack Zipes, *Fairy Tale as Myth/Myth as Fairy Tale* (Lexington: University of Kentucky Press, 1994), 3.

6. Marina Warner, *From the Beast to the Blonde: Fairy Tales and their Tellers* (NY: Farrar, Straus & Giroux, 1995). The female collectors included sisters-in-law of the Grimms and the wife of Andrew Lang.

7. See, e.g., Gail Holst-Warhaft, *Dangerous Voices: Women's Laments in Greek Literature* (NY: Routledge, 1992).

8. Salman Rushdie, *The Wizard of Oz* (London: British Film Institute, 1992), 42.

9. The most accessible introduction to the work of Parry and Lord is Lord's book *The Singer of Tales* (Harvard Univrsity Press, 1960); the second edition, issued in 2000, includes a CD of some of the recordings of Yugoslav bards made by Parry and Lord in the 1930s and by Lord in the 1950s.

10. See, e.g., William G. Thalmann, *The Swineherd and the Bow: Representations of Class in the Odyssey* (Ithaca: Cornell University Press, 1998), and my own *Siren Songs: Gender, Audiences, and Narrators in the Odyssey* (Ann Arbor: University of Michigan Press, 1995).

11. Peter Rose, *Sons of the Gods, Children of Earth: Ideology and Literary Form in Ancient Greece* (Ithaca, NY: Cornell University Press, 1992), ch. 2.

12. Norman O. Brown, *Hermes the Thief: The Evolution of a Myth* (1947; repr. NY: Random House, 1969), 115.

13. An early source is Herodotus 2.134. For details, see the entries 'Aesop' and 'fable' in the *Oxford Classical Dictionary*, 3rd ed., ed. Simon Hornblower and Antony Spawforth (Oxford University Press, 1996).

14. Ioannes Kakridis, 'The Recognition of Odysseus', in *Homer Revisited* (Thessaloniki 1971).

15. For recent evidence of female bards in the Croatian tradition, see Chapter 1 above.

16. Some more recent readings of the *Odyssey* that see it as deliberately exploring the boundaries between archaic Greece and other cultures are François Hartog, *Memories of Odysseus: Frontier Tales from Ancient Greece*, trans. Janet Lloyd (University of Chicago Press, 2001) and Carol Dougherty, *The Raft of Odysseus: The Ethnographic Imagination of Homer's Odyssey* (Oxford University Press, 2001).

17. Zipes, *Fairy Tale as Myth* (above, n. 5), 49.

18. Some examples of narratological studies of Homer are Scott Richardson, *The Homeric Narrator* (Nashville, Tenn.: Vanderbilt University Press, 1990); John Peradotto, *Man in the Middle Voice: Name and Narration in the Odyssey* (Princeton University Press, 1990); and my own *Siren Songs* (n. 10 above).

19. Vladimir Propp, *Morphology of the Folktale*, trans. Laurence Scott (2nd ed. Austin: University of Texas Press, 1968; orig. Russian ed. 1928).

20. Graham Anderson, *Fairytale in the Ancient World* (London: Routledge, 2000), 63-7.

21. John J. Winkler, *Auctor and Actor: A Narratological Reading of Apuleius' Golden Ass* (Berkeley: Univ. of California Press, 1985).

22. This motivation is made explicit in the related Greek novel *Lucius or the Ass*. See William Hansen, ed, *Anthology of Ancient Greek Popular Literature* (Bloomington: Indiana University Press, 1998), 91.

23. Warner (n. 6 above), 279.

24. The 'Quarrel of the Ancients and the Moderns', a debate over the relative merits of classical and contemporary authors, was raging among French intellectuals during this period. Educated women tended to champion the Moderns (as did Charles Perrault, best known to us for his retelling of fairy tales).

25. Warner (n. 6 above), 294.

26. Warner, ch. 18; cf. her essay 'Beautiful Beasts: The Call of the Wild', in *Six Myths of Our Time* (NY: Random House, 1995), 63-81.

27. In *The Bloody Chamber* (1979; repr. Harmondsworth: Penguin, 1981). 'The Courtship of Mr Lyon', in the same volume, is another version of 'Beauty and the Beast'.

28. Nancy Schultz, 'The E-Files', *Washington Post*, 29 April 2001.

29. Cited in Schultz. Jenkins is the author of *Textual Poachers: Television Fans and Participatory Culture* (NY: Routledge, 1992). See also Camille Bacon-Smith, *Enterprising Women: Television Fandom and the Creation of Popular Myth* (Philadelphia: University of Pennsylvania Press, 1992).

Further Reading

What follows is a very short list of readable and accessible works on mythology, most of which are discussed in this book. I have included a few works on myth in visual art, an important topic omitted from the book for want of space.

Bonnefoy, Yves, ed. *Greek and Egyptian Mythologies*. Trans. under the direction of Wendy Doniger. Chicago: University of Chicago Press, 1992. An exciting interpretive overview of Greek and Egyptian mythologies, combining the approaches of Dumézil and Lévi-Strauss.

Brown, Norman O. *Hermes the Thief: The Evolution of a Myth*. NY: Random House, 1947. This old and speculative study remains fascinating reading and a fine example of how awareness of history and social class can enrich the study of myth.

Caldwell, Richard. *The Origin of the Gods: A Psychoanalytic Study of Greek Theogonic Myth*. NY: Oxford University Press, 1989. Includes (in ch. 2) a good summary of Freudian theory applicable to the interpretation of myths.

Carpenter, Thomas H. *Art and Myth in Ancient Greece*. London: Thames & Hudson, 1991. 'An introductory survey of myth as it appears in surviving ancient Greek visual arts created between about 700 and 323 BC'; richly illustrated.

Christ, Carol. *Laughter of Aphrodite: Reflections on a Journey to the Goddess*. San Francisco: Harper & Row, 1987. Eloquent personal testimony of an early proponent of spiritual feminism.

Doniger, Wendy. *Splitting the Difference: Gender and Myth in Ancient Greece and India*. Chicago: University of Chicago Press, 1999. Excellent comparative study, great fun to read.

Dowden, Ken. *The Uses of Greek Mythology*. London: Routledge, 1992. An overview of Greek mythology by a contemporary 'ritualist'.

Edmunds, Lowell, ed. *Approaches to Greek Myth*. Baltimore: Johns Hopkins University Press, 1990. Includes ritual, historical, comparative, structuralist, psychoanalytic, and iconographic approaches. Scholarly but accessible.

Fantham, Elaine, et al. *Women in the Classical World: Image and Text*. NY: Oxford University Press, 1994. Thorough survey of the evidence for the lives of women in ancient Greece and Rome.

Finnegan, Ruth. *Oral Poetry: Its Nature, Significance and Social Context*. Cambridge University Press, 1977. Draws on a vast range of material from many world cultures to argue for the diversity of oral genres and styles.

Foley, Helene, ed. *The Homeric Hymn to Demeter: Translation, Commentary, and Interpretive Essays*. Princeton University Press, 1994. Described in Chapter 1.

Gordon, R.L., ed. *Myth, Religion and Society*. Cambridge University Press, 1981.

A collection of some of the most interesting essays of the French classicists who use structuralist methods.

Grant, Michael. *Myths of the Greeks and Romans*. New York: New American Library, 1962. Still the most readable general introduction to classical myths; combines retellings with a range of theoretical approaches and a deep knowledge of the classical tradition in later art and literature.

Lincoln, Bruce. *Theorizing Myth: Narrative, Ideology, and Scholarship*. University of Chicago Press, 1999. A virtuosic overview of the history of myth interpretation, with a probing analysis of the relationship between myth and scholarship.

Mallory, J.P. *In Search of the Indo-Europeans: Language, Archaeology and Myth*. London: Thames & Hudson, 1989. Thorough, scholarly, but highly readable.

McManus, Barbara F. *Classics and Feminism: Gendering the Classics*. NY: Twayne, 1997. Excellent introduction to the impact of feminism within the discipline of classics.

Penner, Hans, ed. *Teaching Lévi-Strauss*. Atlanta: Scholars Press, 1998. Includes translations of some of Lévi-Strauss' most important essays on myth with a useful introduction and a range of critical appraisals by other scholars.

Petropoulos, John. *Heat and Lust: Hesiod's Midsummer Festival Scene Revisited*. Lanham, MD: Rowman & Littlefield, 1994. Shows how the study of modern Greek folklore can illuminate an ancient text.

Puhvel, Jaan. *Comparative Mythology*. Baltimore: Johns Hopkins University Press, 1987. Clear, readable introduction to Indo-European comparative mythology. Some of the assumptions are a bit dated, especially in the chapter on Greece.

Segal, Robert A. *Theorizing about Myth*. Amherst: University of Massachusetts Press, 1999. Succinct and accessible evaluation and *comparison* of important theories of myth interpretation.

Shapiro, H. Alan. *Myth into Art: Poet and Painter in Classical Greece*. London: Routledge, 1994. An introduction to characteristic differences between the ways in which myths were represented in literature and in visual art.

Tyrrell, William Blake. *Amazons: A Study in Athenian Mythmaking*. Baltimore: Johns Hopkins University Press, 1984. Accessible structuralist analysis of Amazon myths.

Warner, Marina. *From the Beast to the Blonde: On Fairy Tales and Their Tellers*. NY: Farrar, Straus & Giroux, 1995. Traces the history of the modern fairy tale as a women's genre and analyses specific tale-types from a feminist perspective.

———*Six Myths of Our Time: Little Angels, Little Monsters, Beautiful Beasts, and More*. New York: Random House, 1995. Traces the history of specific mythic themes in fairy tales and in late twentieth-century popular culture.

Zipes, Jack. *Fairy Tale as Myth / Myth as Fairy Tale*. Lexington: University Press of Kentucky, 1994. Puts fairy tales (and modern equivalents, such as *The Wizard of Oz*) in their specific historical contexts; warns against their mystification of power relations while praising their 'utopian impulse'. Best read in conjunction with Warner.

Index

189